EARLY PIETY

THE BASIS OF ELEVATED CHARACTER.

A Discourse to the

GRADUATING CLASS OF WESLEYAN UNIVERSITY,

AUGUST, 1850.

By STEPHEN OLIN, D. D., LL. D.

New-York:
PUBLISHED BY LANE & SCOTT,
200 Mulberry-street.
JOSEPH LONGKING, PRINTER.
1851.

EARLY PIETY

THE

BASIS OF ELEVATED CHARACTER.

"I have written unto you, young men, because ye are strong, and the word of God abideth in you, and ye have overcome the wicked one."—1 John ii, 14.

THE Gospel demands of every human being an unreserved consecration of body and soul, with all their energies and capabilities, throughout the entire period of his probation. In thus claiming for God *all* the services which a mortal man, aided by Divine grace, can render, it puts forth a claim upon any peculiar powers, endowments, or faculties with which he may be providentially endowed or intrusted. In asserting its rightful dominion over our entire earthly career, it proclaims the Divine right to reign with an undivided and unrivalled authority over each period of life. Every talent is confided to us under the tacit condition that it shall be used and improved in accordance with the will and design of the great Giver. Days, and months, and years, are added to our existence here below, because they supply us with more opportunities and advantages for working out our own salvation, and promoting the well-being of others; for building up the kingdom of Christ, and making manifest the glory of God. For the attainment of these high ends, much reliance is placed upon human exertion, and the physical and intellectual resources of every age and station are tasked to the uttermost. Even the morning of existence, and the childhood of religious life, are pressed into this great enterprise. "I write unto you, little children, because your sins are forgiven you for His name's sake." The glow, and out-bursting, joyous gratitude of the new-born soul—the fervours of his "first love"—the fresh lustre of his "beautiful garments," become potent agencies for good, and no more pleasant incense than his ever rises up to Heaven.

The mature piety and deep acquaintance with Divine things, which are the result of long experience and habitual communion with God, also have their special vocation under the Gospel economy. "I write unto you, fathers, because you know Him that is from the beginning." These "old disciples" constitute the link of connexion between the existing Christian Church and the Church of history, as well as between the Church militant and the Church triumphant. They are the channels through which the tide of spiritual life has flowed down upon us from the ages of the past. They are the depositaries of reverend traditions, and the conservators and models of orthodoxy in opinion and purity of life. Without being conscious of exercising so high a function, they have made the Church what it is. Our Christianity, with all its excellencies as well as its imperfections, has been derived from theirs. It has, no doubt, undergone some modifications. It has, in some respects, deteriorated in our hands. In others, it has grown better; but, as a whole, it is a natural and fair derivation from the waning Christian age, to which a new and vigorous religious generation are rapidly succeeding. We sometimes unconsciously look upon the company of venerable disciples who move in the van of our heavenward march, as having really, and to all important ends, accomplished their warfare and won the victory. Should all others forsake the Saviour, they, we feel quite sure, will never participate in the crime; for they have lived unto God till religion has, through grace, become a sort of second nature, in which all their habits, and sentiments, and aspirations, and joys have their source and support. To turn them away from God and the heavenly inheritance must require some great moral convulsion. It would be like the annulment of the law of gravitation—like thrusting a rolling planet from its appointed orb. We do not subscribe to the inamissibility of grace, and the inevitable salvation of all souls once regenerated,—and yet we firmly believe that these fathers and mothers in Israel will never fall. They will abide in the old paths, whoever turns back. They remember the days of old. They "know Him that is from the beginning." So long, at least, as *they* live, there will be true witnesses. Their trumpet shall give a certain sound. They are living epistles of Christ, which shall continue to be read of all men. So long as they constitute a part of the life of the Church, the Church cannot lose its vitality. While their presence and prayers among us will certainly conciliate the Divine favour, and perpetuate a holy seed, they reprove our backslidings, and warn us of dangers, and recall us to the old landmarks of truth, and experience, and duty.

Let us thank God for so bright a manifestation of his grace in the fathers, who still bless and guide us by their counsels, and in the yet larger company of mature, established Christians who still bear the burden and heat of the day. We may yet rejoice in their light for a season, and there will be days of mourning when these luminaries, so long our guides and exemplars, shall one after another be exalted to shed their radiance upon brighter, holier regions. It will, however, readily occur to the thoughtful hearer, that the high qualities, in virtue of which aged, mature Christians fulfil for the church offices so conservative and salutary, are partially or wholly incompatible with the performance of other functions connected no less intimately with the spread and efficacy of the Gospel. Conservatism, which spontaneously clings to the past, is less favourable to progress. Zeal for traditional or hereditary opinions or usages is often indiscriminate, and is prone to resist not rash innovations and pernicious novelties alone, but needful improvements. It is no slight calamity that befalls religion and human society, when venerable truths and ancient institutions are guarded with a morbid jealousy, which rejects new discoveries and salutary changes. The Church, under such unpropitious circumstances, is in danger of losing its power and vitality, and of wasting its energies in idle contests for dogmas and forms, which, however true or Scriptural, are no longer of any special significance or utility, now that their life and spirit have departed from them. And here we have occasion to adore the infinite wisdom of the great Head of the Church, in employing for its edification such a variety of gifts and agencies. Under His wonderful economy, men of all ranks and capacities co-operate harmoniously for the production of a common result, each fulfilling his own special and appropriate function, and, at the same time, supplying some deficiency, or checking some exaggerated action of his fellow-labourer. The rich and the poor have assigned to them their proper spheres, and they contribute not alike, but equally, it may be, to the general weal. The faith, and prayers, and spotless example of an illiterate or obscure man may promote as successfully the great designs of Christianity as the counsels of the sage or the eloquence of the learned. Thus it is that "the whole body, fitly joined together, and compacted by that which every joint supplieth, according to the effectual working in the measure of every part, maketh increase of the body unto the edifying itself in love."

For the satisfaction of wants and liabilities which find no adequate provision in the fixed ideas and unyielding habits of veteran piety, the Gospel makes its appeal to the special endowments and adaptations of the young. "I have written to you, young men, because ye are strong, and the word of God abideth in you, and ye have overcome the wicked one." In the economy of Divine Providence, youth is endowed with peculiar attributes, on which the success of all great moral and social interests and enterprises is made dependent.

I. This responsibility for the well-being of the race, which accrues to the young in virtue of their providential endowments, is devolved upon them by an inevitable destiny. They are the predestined successors of all who now wield moral influence, and all who occupy positions of authority and power. They are moving incessantly onward toward this great inheritance, and the flight of years makes haste to bring them into contact with burdens and responsibilities which they cannot elude or devolve upon others. Those who are now young *must* govern mankind. They *must* become the teachers of the race. They must become the world's lawgivers, and its dispensers of justice. They must manage its material interests—must plan and prosecute its improvements and ameliorations—must conduct its wars and negotiations—must meet the unseen exigencies of the great future. God has provided no other teachers for that coming generation, which, in its turn, is destined to occupy this great field of action and probation, and to transmit to a still later posterity its character—its virtues, and vices, and achievements. Were we able to divest this great law of human existence of its inefficiency as a hackneyed truism, and clothe it in the freshness and potency of a newly-discovered truth, we should need no other argument to impress upon the young the duty of diligence and faithfulness in their high vocation; for the young, though often rash and reckless of the future, are neither selfish nor malevolent. They would not thrust themselves upon the inheritance in reserve for them without qualifications to preserve and improve it. They would not bring back upon the world the ignorance of the dark ages, nor reproduce upon the face of civilized society the horrible scenes of the reign of terror.

They would not tarnish the lustre of our national character by deeds of cowardice, treachery, or dishonour. They would not give to the country a race of incompetent or profligate statesmen. They would recoil from the thought of occupying the pulpits of this Christian land, the strongholds of its morality and stern virtues, without the requisite qualifications of intelligence and piety. They would not dwarf and taint the public mind with a feeble, polluted literature, nor degrade the schools and liberal professions to which this great republic looks for the men of the future—its orators, its teachers, the guides of its youth, and the leaders of its senates. And yet nothing is more certain than that these great interests, one and all, look to the present generation of young men as their sole hope and resource. Nothing is less a matter of doubt than that these potent agencies, on which the well-being of a great nation depends, must speedily come under the direction of the young men who are now forming their character, moral and intellectual, in our schools and colleges—many of them wholly unconcerned about that future in which they have so deep a stake, and for which they will be held to a responsibility so fearful.

We should place before the youth of this land only a very humble standard of duty and ambition in urging them to such attainments as will merely enable them to maintain these institutions and social and moral enterprises in their present state of efficiency and usefulness. To do less than this would plainly be nothing less than treason against our country and common humanity. It cost our fathers infinite toil and sacrifices, and precious blood, to raise this country to its present position, and to form such a heritage of light, and liberty, and glory as they are ready to bequeath to their sons; and that young man must be dead to all high aspirations who does not burn with shame at the thought of transmitting it to posterity enfeebled, or dilapidated. One or two such recreant generations would plunge this free and glorious land into the darkness and wretchedness of its primitive barbarism, and make themselves the reproach of noble ancestors, and the scorn and byword of history.

But the rising generation cannot even escape this foul dishonour of wasting its inheritance, and betraying the sacred interests intrusted to it for the benefit of posterity, without high attainments in knowledge and virtue. Our forefathers were a brave, intellectual, noble race; and they who now sway the destinies of this country are educated, vigorous, laborious, enterprising men. The land is no doubt cursed with hordes of demagogues and pretenders, and its honours are too often bestowed upon the unworthy and incompetent. Still, the great body of our legislators, public officers, and professional men, are not deficient either in literary attainments or intellectual vigour. There is a Vulcanic energy at work in our enterprises of science, and fabrication, and internal improvement. A mighty intellectual machinery is concerned in bringing forth the products of our vast literature, periodical and permanent. Many thousand of fine minds, and well cultivated, are labouring incessantly and intensely in our pulpits and schools of learning, to promote the moral and mental illumination of the people of this great country.

We must not undervalue the past, or complain unjustly of the deficiencies of the present time. Our country has been made what it is, and is kept up to its actual high moral and social position, by the strenuous exertion of immense capacities and honourable virtues. It will be no easy task for our young men to outstrip their predecessors. It will even be well for them if they shall be prepared to act the part which awaits them without provoking unfavourable comparisons—if they shall acquit themselves as well in the sight of their country, of history, and of God.

Something more than this, however, will justly be expected of them. It is the glory of the men of the present generation that they have improved upon all past ages, and greatly enriched and beautified the inheritance which their fathers bequeathed them. It will be the undying reproach of their successors if this full tide of improvement shall be stayed upon their accession to the high places of power and responsibility. They will enter upon their career with peculiar advantages. The accumulations of past ages will be their resources for new enterprises. The light of rich and varied experiments shines full upon their pathway, and the wonderful discoveries of the last half century constitute the vantage-ground from which they are allowed to commence their new career. If with facilities so many and so great, unknown to their predecessors, they shall do no more than maintain the actual status of the intelligence, and happiness, and virtue of the community, they are destined to act but an inglorious part. They ought to contribute to the welfare of society such measures of new light, and vivacity, and momentum, as will quicken and multiply the energies of every ameliorating enterprise. This is their proper function and vocation, for which they should diligently equip themselves, as champions whose eyes are already fixed upon the arena of the coming conflict.

The actual state of education, morals, and happiness in a community, may be regarded as the true expression of the power of the moral and intellectual forces engaged for its improvement. The efficiency and usefulness of a Church, for instance, are precisely what the zeal, purity, and intelligence of its members can make it. We may conclude, therefore, that the Christian enterprises of the present time must remain stationary, without some new accession of moral resources. If the rising generation shall come forward with only the same degrees of piety and intelligence that belong to their fathers, then the utmost that can be expected is, that the cause of religion and humanity shall not retrograde. Progress, under the circumstances supposed, is wholly out of the question. The Church is now barely able to hold its ground against the opposing forces of sin and error, or to advance with a tardy step to future triumphs; and if it is to be recruited and reinforced by such members and ministers only as already wield its destinies, it must remain in essentially the same condition, while the accession of even a few persons of deeper piety, and stronger faith, and larger views, might sweep away the obstacles that retard its progress, and open a career of unexampled successes. A single individual of enlarged conceptions of

2

duty, and burning zeal for Christ, is sometimes able to communicate new spirit to a whole Church which has, for years, scarcely given a sign of vitality. It had just enough of moral power to maintain a bare existence, and resist the pressure from without; and now the additional impetus given by one true man of God puts everything in motion and triumphs over obstacles. What victories, then, might we not anticipate, what enlargement for Zion, could the whole host of our young men be induced to gird themselves with strength, and enter upon the whitening field to which they are called, with something like the spirit of primitive Christianity? It would be as a new life from the dead. It would be as the birth of a new dispensation. They who are ready to perish would revive again, and all the islands of the sea would rejoice.

Manifestly it is such a revival of heavenly charity, and wisdom, and apostolic zeal, that is imperatively demanded by the present condition of all our social and Christian enterprises. The passing era will ever be recognised in history as an age of noble conceptions and of great moral convictions. It has planned, and begun to execute, godlike enterprises, but it evidently lacks the sinews needful for their successful accomplishments. It reels under the burdens it has assumed. The existing race of Christians has propagated sublime ideas, which it is appointed for their successors to realize in sublime achievements. This is in accordance with a great law. An age of discovery leads in an age of performance. First comes the science, and then its applications to life. The Church is well furnished with grand ideas. It has on its hands comprehensive evangelizing schemes, whose successful accomplishment will usher in the millennium. What she now wants is agents to execute them. She wants an army of young men, large-minded and large-hearted, and deeply baptized into the Saviour's spirit. This is the great want to which all others are subordinate. Let it be supplied, and all other obstacles will vanish away. The cause of Christ and humanity calls for men—needs men—cultivated, sanctified, self-sacrificing, brave men, and it really wants nothing else to the completeness of its triumphs. Material resources with which the Church overflows, only wait for the bidding of lips touched with holy fire to call them forth for the sacrifice. And now what Christian young man will endure the thought, that all these goodly enterprises for the improvement and salvation of the race shall fail or languish for want of worthy champions? The Church has just now started forth from the ignominious repose of centuries, and trembles to recognise itself as charged by Christ with the evangelization of the world. Shall this work, so nobly begun, fail or languish for want of labourers? Is it tolerable to think of, that the triumph of Christ shall be postponed, and the deadly curse of sin continue to blight the hopes of three-fourths of the human race, because we love our ease and our money, and because our young men have shallow piety and huge ambition? We have discovered that the general diffusion of a more thorough and effective education is absolutely indispensable for a self-governing people, and that whatever else our republic has or lacks, the preservation of freedom and happiness without this great reform is an impossibility. The work is already begun, and the means for its extension and completion are at least partially provided. Will our young men accept of this holy trust at the hands of their fathers? Are they ready to offer themselves for a service equally commended to their favour by religion and patriotism? Good men, who are yet alive, were the first to know and proclaim that the exhilarating bowl, which fashion had long made indispensable in the high places of society, and appetite had made the tyrant and the scourge of common life—which was fondly kissed by ruby lips, and inspired the eloquence of grave ecclesiastics, is an accursed poisoned chalice, which has drugged our people with disease, and vice, and damning guilt. This fearful truth had nearly succeeded in penetrating the heart of our population, and making its lodgment in the public conscience, when, through the weariness of some of its advocates, and the indiscretions of others, the apathy of the Church, and the sleepless efforts of interested dealers, their deluded victims, and demagogue abettors, a paralyzing reaction has befallen the great enterprise, and the polluting cup is again brought forth from its hiding-place—again sparkles at the feast, and maddens the joyous circle of our youth. Are our educated young men prepared to preach up another crusade, and march in the van of another holy war against this worse than the false prophet? Our own favoured land, and the entire Christian world, unquestionably labour under great and grievous social evils. Our intense and highly artificial civilization does in some of its modes and operations, press with dreadful and almost exterminating severity upon the happiness, the hopes, and the virtues of large classes of the people. Ignorant quacks, and interested pretenders and demagogues, are everywhere prescribing absurd and pernicious remedies for this inveterate disease. Religion and education possess the true panacea, and they would enlist an army of valiant, wise philanthropists in an enterprise which must fail in ordinary hands. Are our young men ready for this good work also? Will this call to holy duties be able to make itself heard amid the incitements to selfishness and ambition which throng the avenues to professional and public life?

For the satisfaction of these, and other moral and social wants, which press so heavily upon our country and the human race, intelligent, pious young men are at this moment the only adequate resource. Others, who have a heart for such work, are already occupied, and their energies are already fully tasked in maintaining these great moral enterprises in their actual state of advancement. They look to the young for the succour without which reaction and ignominious retrogression will be unavoidable. They boldly confront the foe and keep him at bay, whilst, with every muscle strained, they beckon to their sons to "come and help them."

Young men alone can be fully adapted to the special exigencies of their own times. Those who have been long engaged in any department of action acquire habits favourable to success in their particular pursuit, which often become disqualifications under a change of circumstances, or for new enterprises. The middle-aged pastor will generally be found essentially unfit for the new duties and ideas of missionary life. He cannot learn strange languages, and inure himself to new climates and modes of life. The young man, on the contrary, has nothing to unlearn. He is pliable and plastic, ready to be moulded into any form of physical and mental activity which the exigencies of the times may demand. When the French revolution had brought on a crisis in human affairs unknown in the world's previous history, old statesmen and old generals were found universally unfit for the new exigency, and supreme power, civil and military, passed, as if in obedience to some hidden law, to the vigorous hands of Napoleon, and Pitt, and Talleyrand, and Wellington, all young men, who took their character from the crisis, and in their turn impressed it upon the times. Several of our great benevolent enterprises, which are rapidly extending their influences to the remotest nations of the earth, were projected by young men, while they were still undergraduates; and Mills, and Judson, and Newell, passed immediately from the schools into the distant lands where they laid the foundations of Christian empires. Young men have usually been Heaven's chosen depositaries of new and great ideas, and its chosen instruments for effecting beneficent revolutions. They soonest hear, and most deeply feel, the appeals of suffering humanity, and their character most readily conforms itself to the hue and pressure of their era.

For prudent counsels, and the conduct of grave negotiations, for the conservation of holy truths and time-honoured institutions, for the safe management of the great trusts and established interests of human society, we are to look to the serene, unimpassioned wisdom of more advanced life; but new and difficult enterprises, and daring moral adventures that are without precedent in the memory of the aged, must, for the most part, expect to enlist their champions from the ranks of buoyant, unhackneyed youth. This is eminently the period of mental and bodily vigour and power. The warm blood courses bravely through the veins, and every limb and muscle rejoices in action. The bosom swells with high hopes, which disappointment has not yet chilled with its paralyzing touch. The young are wont to place confidence in man, in human improvement, in truth, and in the power of endeavour. Experience has not yet made them timid, nor broken the spirit of adventure. The future rises up before them gorgeous with rich promise, and opulent in hidden resources. Religion chastens, but it does not dim these vivid conceptions and lofty aspirations of the young. Very often, indeed, the discoveries of faith far outstrip and outshine the visions of fancy; and what was sheer extravagance in the expectations of the natural man, becomes an object of sober and reasonable pursuit with him who has received an endowment of strength from on high. It is a great point gained when we can get young men, constitutionally prone to adventure and activity, who love labour, and fear nothing—whose bounding hearts impel them onward, as if conscious that to will and to achieve were tasks equally practicable—it is a great thing to get all these elements of efficiency fairly embarked in some holy enterprise in which the smallest degrees of success might satisfy the most ardent ambition, and the grandeur and certainty of whose triumphs can sustain the spirit of man under all the vicissitudes of hope deferred. Here is found precisely that conjunction of circumstances which is most favourable to the highest development of the best qualities of the heart and the intellect. The inspiration of an object divinely sublime, and yet in closest contact with all the benevolent feelings; the prospect of a glorious reward, acting without prejudice to conscious, disinterested philanthrophy—infallible guarantees of ultimate, complete success—offer a combination of motives that cannot fail to exalt the human powers to their utmost capacity, and even to make ordinary men great.

In addition to the inspiration of ennobling pursuits acting upon the plastic nature and fervent temperament of fresh and buoyant life, Christianity furnishes to young men other and peculiar elements of strength. "*The word of God abideth in them,*" and they are thus supplied, from the beginning of their career, with rules of action and maxims of life perfectly adapted to all their circumstances and wants. It is not necessary to prove that the Bible, which is the expression of Divine wisdom, announces to man the true method of life. It contains the mind of God, and makes known to us the decisions of the highest intelligence. In all matters of high moral import it *reveals* to us, in anticipation of experience, those great practical lessons which cannot be learned elsewhere, if at all, but by years of careful observation and laborious experiment. Wisdom acquired by methods so tedious and expensive, usually comes too late for any valuable purpose, after life has been exhausted in fruitless, misdirected endeavours, and its energies have been impaired, and the heart saddened by discouragement and discomfiture. Life commenced and prosecuted under the infallible guidance of the Divine oracles, escapes all such retarding influences. Its movements *begin* in the right direction. Its energies are saved from the wear and the waste of unsuccessful essays and of an endless empiricism. The character early acquires compactness and solidity, and that momentum which is derived from fixedness of purpose and singleness of heart.

There is great advantage also in the Divine authority of the rules which religion prescribes for the conduct of life. Its announcements are so many of the decrees of Jehovah, of which it is not in human folly to question the wisdom, and to which nothing short of absolute madness could hope to offer successful resistance. Obedience, therefore, becomes the highest dictate of reason as well as of conscience. All the interests of time and eternity are involved in a frank, earnest concurrence with these expressions of the Divine will. After God has spoken, there are no doubtful questions to settle—no wavering probabilities for scrutiny and adjustment. It only remains for those who have heard his voice to gird up their loins and hasten to the accomplishment of an appointed task. It must be obvious to the slightest reflection how much the business of life is simplified by this authoritative settlement of doubtful questions, and the subordination of all its pursuits to one controlling principle. They who choose to follow other guides, necessarily lose this powerful element of efficiency. They must often hesitate in the choice of their rules of action—they must often falter in the pursuits to which they finally devote themselves, and often fail in the attainment of their objects, through the insufficiency of worldly motives to sustain untiring activity. They hang in equipoise, while others, obedient to the Divine lawgiver, advance in the race. They stop to reconsider where the demand is strongest for accelerated motion. They find the incentives to which they have yielded up the direction of life too feeble to sustain them. They doubt, under the pressure of toil and weariness, whether they have not consulted ambition and avarice at the sacrifice of higher interests—whether they may not have thought too little of the claims of repose, or too highly of reputation. They discover, too late, some lack of congeniality for the scenes or society upon which they have been precipitated by levity, or pride, or indolence. Above all, will the thought that God is not in all their schemes, and that they tend to an issue upon which Heaven's blessing has never been asked nor promised, often obtrude itself, to relax the sinews of effort, and even to sadden the triumphs of success. Such misgivings are most likely to come upon the mind in its days of doubt and despondency, when the hand is tremulous and the heart faint. Just then it is that the Christian most feels the support of his principles. "The word of God abideth in him," and he travels on "from strength to strength." It is his infallible counsellor in a time of perplexity. It assures him of deliverance from all dangers and all disasters. It sustains him most completely when all other supports confess their insufficiency. Its light is most intense in the darkest day, and it raises the loudest notes of victory when its devoted champions are borne on their shields from the mortal conflict.

The Christian young man gains another element of efficiency in the permanence of the influences under which his character is formed,—"The word of God *abideth* in him." From youth to old age, through all of life's changes, he walks by the same unerring light. His eye is fixed upon one object. His pursuits obey one great law, and all tend to a common grand result. Life's entire energies are concentrated upon a point which becomes henceforth the goal of all his efforts and aspirations. Lower worldly maxims lose their force and application with the progress and mutations of time. The appetite becomes sated with enjoyment or paralyzed by age. Disappointment, or the sober second thought of experience, dissipates the illusions of ambition. Hardly any worldly motive but avarice, confessedly the lowest and the worst, is accustomed to maintain its sway to the close of life. Failure, or change in the ruling principle, necessarily destroys unity and continuity of action; and enterprises eagerly begun in the thoughtlessness of youth, are abandoned as hopeless or unworthy by sober manhood. The tastes fluctuate. Imagination refuses any longer to gild the phantom with which it at first seduced the unwary.

With these changes come changes of purpose, and even middle life finds itself unsettled and wavering, shorn of its strength in its very prime and unwasted vigour; while the latter days of an irreligious life are almost invariably tasteless, unsatisfactory, and to all the higher ends of existence absolutely useless. Such a life has, and can have, no pervading unity. Its efforts are unsteady and fitful, as they needs must be from the variable and conflicting impulses of which they are the result. How different the history of him who has chosen God for his portion in early life, and made the Divine will his one rule of action! "The word of God, which abideth in him," is "quick and powerful," and ministers an unfailing supply of living, powerful resources. It has a rule of action and a ministration of strong impulses for each period and exigency of our earthly existence. Buoyant youth and sober manhood it links together in an indissoluble unity of interest, and hope, and effort; and it quickens the slow pulses of hoary age with prospects more radiant and exhilarating than ever rose before the visions of childhood. Now it is chiefly in this steady and unfaltering devotion of the entire life to a single object, that we are to look for the secret of all eminent success. It was to this continuity and intensity of effort in a single direction, rather than to any special attributes of genius, that Davy, and Cuvier, and others, were indebted for their eminent achievements in science. For the production of great characters or great actions, there is wanted the early adoption of some worthy object of pursuit—its steady prosecution through all the vicissitudes of life—and an earnest, fervent temperament, which stirs old age itself with living impulses. How completely religion, embraced in early life, satisfies these indispensable conditions, we have already seen.

The presence and supremacy of Divine truth, which pervades the life with an influence so benignant, and produces such strength of character and efficiency of action, performs for the young another function very noticeable and important. It offers itself as a guide and counsellor at a period of life when there exists the strongest indisposition to listen to human advisers, and when submission to human authority is often deemed incompatible with a manly independence. This tendency to revolt against the admonitions of age and experience, is among the most unaccountable of the characteristics of young persons —especially of those who are early removed from parental control. Every teacher finds in it a chief obstacle in the way of a satisfactory discharge of his duties, and it often proves a fatal barrier to that moral and mental culture which is the proper business of education. Our reference here is not to that reckless folly peculiar to low and vicious dispositions, which makes a pastime of perpetrating petty crimes and violating good order, and slides into vulgar profligacy through the spontaneous tendencies of a base and intractable nature. Youths of a more ingenuous character, by no means deficient in good impulses and manly aspirations, often fall into the delusion of regarding obedience, and all manifestations of deference for age and authority, as some reflection upon their dignity, and an indication of a tame and timid spirit. They place *their point of honour* in violating the order which would protect their retired hours from intrusion, and in contemning the solicitude and counsels that would encourage and guide to mental improvement, and conserve their moral sentiments and character. They avoid, as a reproach and a stigma, all suspicion of recognising the restraints and reverencing the ordinances of religion. They are ashamed of having it thought that they bear with them some respect for the holy influences of home recollections and sympathies—some tender remembrance of mother and sisters—some dutiful reverence for the authority and instructions of a father. This false honour and false shame too often tyrannize over conscience and the heart—prove too strong for the love of knowledge and distinction—too strong for the restraints of law and morality. I have seen fine young men, endowed with genius and high aspirations, in whom this absurd, unnatural controversy with their own real sentiments, as well as interests, had assumed the form of a monomania, directed against every influence solicitous to promote their well-being, and restrain them from recklessness. More distressing cases never occur than such as leave no power for good but in a rigid exercise of authority—a remedy little adapted to cure, though it may sometimes restrain the folly which so pertinaciously revolts against influence, and thinks it dishonour to listen to good advice. Religion offers the only remedy, and, in certain temperaments, the early inculcation of its principles constitutes the only preventive of the unmanageable evil under consideration. The fear of God, once established in the mind, will often prove an effectual antidote to the bad independence which denies respect to age and allegiance to authority. The most vaulting ambition may not deem it a degradation to do homage to Jehovah. The perverted sentiment of honour which spurns the advice of teacher and parent, may yet acknowledge that God's counsels are worthy of some respect. The pride that cannot stoop to confess a fault, or to avow purposes of amendment, may consent to bow in submission to an authority which is confessedly supreme, and to do homage to a power too high to provoke envy, or to tolerate disobedience.

The revival of early religious impressions has saved many a reckless youth, who obstinately refused to be guided by any human authority or influence. The dupes of bad example and perverted sentiments of honour sometimes discover, with surprise, that their awakened deference for Divine authority has, without provoking jealousy, or wounding their self-love, brought them into perfect harmony with laws and restraints against which it had been their pride and their business to wage perpetual war. It may be affirmed, without qualification, that there is always hope for a young man in whom the great truths of religion have made an early lodgement. They have a tenacity of life beyond what we are accustomed to think of. "The word of God abideth" in the instructed son of Christian parents, and makes disclosure of its latent energies at times and in ways which we least of all anticipate. It whispers good counsel, and utters notes of warning in hearts apparently dead to its influences, and into ears contemptuously closed against the most faithful admonitions. How often have our unbelieving fears in regard to thoughtless, reckless youth been signally rebuked by their sudden and unexpected conversion! How often have we seen the graces of a backslidden young man revived again, after years of neglect and apparent indifference to Divine things! If we are compelled to admit that some cast off the restraints of early education, and even of a religious profession, and apparently " make shipwreck of their faith," we are also bound to acknowledge, for the honour of Divine grace, that a large proportion of them turn again to righteousness. Some good, reviving influence from heaven visits them. Some array of affecting circumstances—some hour like this, when tender remembrances come up to mingle with the fears and hopes of the future—perhaps the thoughtfulness which an actual entrance upon serious, active life forces upon them, is made the occasion of a recurrence to holy first principles. The slumbering elements of eternal truth then awaken into new life. Repudiated conscience trembles into new consciousness and power. The tender associations of childhood and home—the mother's tear—the family altar—the joyous, holy experiences of Christian fellowship and heavenly hopes, rise up before the soul's eye with the energy of a Divine resurrection. All honour to the powerful word, which through so many dark months and years slept, but did not die, in these returning souls. "The word of God abideth in them," and is likely, some day, to make its power known. So strong is the evidence of past experience on this point, that I always *expect* young men, who have been piously trained, to be converted. I expect to hear, if I do not personally witness it, that they who for a time yielded to worldly influences and strong temptations, to the dishonour of their Christian profession, have returned again to Zion with songs; and my reliance for all this is in the vitality and Divine potency of "the word of God." They *may* reject it altogether, but I rather expect impressions so early, so deep, and so Divine, to remain permanent and effectual for saving ends.

Christian young men have won, through the gospel, another victory. They have "overcome the wicked one." He secures a mighty advantage for life's entire career, who, at the outset, solves the great problem of his existence. The conflict between good and evil, in which the greater number of men pass all their days on earth, has formed a fruitful theme for moralists and theologians, Pagan and Christian, ever since the phenomena of man's intellectual and moral nature became objects of research and observation. Some of the earlier Christian sects, as well as some schools of heathen philosophy, believed in the existence of two great principles, a good and an evil principle, engaged in a perpetual conflict for dominion over the universe and in the heart of man. Human life was exhausted in this terrible struggle, and its happiness or misery was very exactly proportioned to the relative ascendency of these warring elements. The undecided strife was thought to be often transferred to a future state of being, when other ages of undefined duration were spent by the soul in struggling onward to its ultimate destiny. This theory expresses very accurately the usual history of man's interior life. It does not exaggerate the fierceness of the protracted contest here, and only errs when it concedes to the hapless victim of an unequal fate another trial beyond the boundaries of the present life. The Gospel adopts this idea of human life in a modified form. The sore conflict is carried on, not between two demons, but between God's holy law and the sinful dispositions of man. It may be prolonged to the hour of death, but no "device or work" is done in the region beyond. It *may* be brought to a successful termination in early life, and even "young men" "have often overcome the wicked one." The true Christian idea of this inner conflict is expressed by St. Paul: "The flesh lusteth against the spirit, and the spirit against the flesh." Early piety puts an end to this doubtful strife, and leaves the young man free to enter, with an undivided heart, and untainted principles, upon the high moral vocation to which his whole existence is consecrated, with no evil habits to unlearn —no counteracting forces to resist—no internal insurrections to suppress beyond the infirmities of a fallen, but renovated nature. A career of virtue and usefulness, commenced under such auspices, has the fairest promise of certain, eminent, complete success. Whoever begins life without a settlement of this great preliminary question, with an unsubdued enemy ambushing his every step, has but two possible alternatives before him. He must either yield himself unresistingly to the foe, and consent to the forfeiture of life's great ends, or, what is more usual, spend his resources in an endless, bootless conflict, under conditions that render victory impossible, and deprive partial success of all its value. He writhes in a consuming fire, which, though sometimes smothered, is never extinguished. He never "overcomes the wicked one," nor ever attempts so much, but only to keep him at bay. He is, consequently, forever in the midst of the conflict of appetite and passion, but never clears his path of enemies farther onward than he can reach with the point of his sword. His life is spent in alternately rolling up the stone of Sisyphus, and starting back from its inevitable recoil. As he does not aim at being a thoroughly good man, real improvement is impossible, and partial reforms only serve to mark his varying gradations in vice. Meantime, his moral diathesis becomes more and more deplorable, by the lowering of his principles, by the growing obtuseness of his moral sentiments, and by the imperceptible formation of habits that strengthen the tendency to evil by something like the sanction of an organic law. The sort of moral progress which we are attempting to portray is illustrated by familiar phenomena of a student's life.

The ingenuous youth, who holds himself obliged in cônscience, and in all manliness, to make the best use of his opportunities for improvement, soon finds the performance of his duties easy and agreeable. Every day's industry and perseverance add to the facility and comfort of his progress, and he speedily attains to such feelings and habits that it would cost him a struggle to omit a duty.

An hour spent in sleep, which ought to be devoted to improvement, wounds his self-respect, and really becomes a source of more annoyance than all the mental efforts of a month's toil in the study and the recitation-room. Such a student, it is obvious, must soon find himself within the range and action of impulses that ensure the highest mental improvement, while they quite disarm all petty temptations to indolence and irregularity. Another enters upon the scholastic career with lower, though not with dishonourable aims. He satisfies his sense of obligation and self-respect by such a performance of scholastic tasks, and such attention to order, as may leave a convenient margin for self-indulgence, and yet not be quite incompatible with proficiency and respectability. This theory of the student-life seldom fails to produce in practice an abundant growth of evils, and to lead to the ultimate forfeiture of the chief benefits of education. As some duties are to be neglected, each, in its turn, becomes a candidate for repudiation. As some liberties are to be taken, the mind is thrown upon the comparison of all minor irregularities, in order to make its selection judicious in number and kind—in time and degree. A few months passed under the auspices of such a code of scholastic morals usually stamp their complexion upon the whole college-life. The indolence and the irregularity, from being occasional, become habitual. They come to be regarded as privileges and enjoyments, and studious industry a burden and a bondage. What can be wrested from the claims of industry and order is won for pleasure and social enjoyments, the rest is a painful sacrifice to necessity. In the end, the performance of duty inflicts a pang, and the period of education becomes a weariness to the flesh, too often a preparatory discipline for an unsuccessful, unhonoured subsequent career.

An illustration borrowed from moral, rather than the mental, aberrations, inculcates the same lesson in another form. A young man leaves the safeguards of home and of parental supervision, alive to all the seductions that beset his new and exposed career, and ambitious of forming a pure and lofty character. It is a wise, and not an unusual, measure of precaution which he adopts, when he arms himself with high resolves, and sometimes with a formal pledge, against every approach toward deadly evils, from which he is purposed to keep his morals pure. From every circle and every incitement which might lead to the violation of his vow he stands aloof, and writes *accursed* upon each inebriating cup. In this position he stands secure, defended by an impregnable bulwark. He "has overcome the wicked one" by a single manly resolve. Appetite itself quails before decision of purpose, and the brave youth pursues the quiet tenor of his way, hardly more exposed to the vice of intemperance than to commit theft or suicide. His associate is skeptical in regard to the danger, and scorns the cowardly precaution against himself. He does not intend to be intemperate, and still less to betray a suspicion of the strength of his own virtue. He will naturally test the value of his reserved rights by their occasional exercise. Bashfully at first, infrequently, stealthily, and only on fit occasions, and in reputable company, does he become initiated into mysteries over which not songs and merry conceits alone shall be poured forth, but bitter tears and unavailing penitence. The restraints, meantime, which respect for public opinion or the dread of exposure impose, and the reproaches of a condemning conscience, constitute a serious drawback upon the pleasure of unlawful indulgence, while the ever-sinking scale of virtue, which honour, fear, and shame incite him to uphold, is maintained at its actual elevation by efforts of self-denial a thousand times more difficult and painful than it would cost to smite down the demon appetite, and at once deliver the falling spirit from its degrading bondage. It should be remembered, too, that this struggle to keep out of the lower depths of degrading vices by those who, in spite of all warning, resolve to disport themselves along the steep declivities that lead to the inevitable abyss, is not a struggle for virtue, nor entitled to any of its immunities or rewards. Every manly effort to break away from the power of a bad habit, and ascend to the dignity of a pure life, is likely to improve the moral sentiments, and evolve some new moral force. Such an *attempt*, made in the integrity of the soul, always has in it a redeeming element, and even unsuccessful efforts, a thousand times repeated in the same spirit, never wholly lose their virtuous character. But he who proposes to do homage to honesty, or temperance, or chastity, or truth, or any other virtue, *to a certain extent only*, commits a crime against all real virtue by the hybrid conception. He fairly takes upon his conscience the guilt of all the degrees of vice from which a selfish prudence alone restrains him ; and we may be sure that he only waits to obtain the consent of some low interest, or to secure guarantees or indemnity against some anticipated injury, in order to do all the evil from which any motive lower than the fear of God and the love of righteousness now restrains him. Of all the villanies committed under the sun, we most indignantly condemn the cautious, well-considered devices of a cool, forecasting man, who aims to secure just so many of the gains of dishonesty as he can, and escape the disgrace and the penalty of detection. The morality of this righteous judgment is justly applicable to all those whose theory of life allows them to stop in the career of virtue whenever it becomes too rough and arduous, and to drink of the cup of vice till they get too strong a taste of its nauseous or its poisonous dregs. These are bad men—not only to the full extent of all the virtues which they discard on vicious principles, but also by the full measure of those which they practise from low and corrupt motives—not only to the extent of all the vices in which they unscrupulously indulge, but also by the whole number and degree of those which their hearts approve, and from which they reluctantly refrain from no higher sentiment than cowardice or cunning. In the sight of God, and of sound ethics, there is no such thing as partial virtue or piety in the man who has resolved to reserve to himself the practice of certain degrees of vice or sin, such as he may deem consistent with convenience or a good name. It is no doubt highly expedient to sin with moderation. Unlawful pleasure may be prolonged by subtracting some degrees from its intensity. They who never even aspire to "overcome the wicked one," may have good reasons for subjecting his acknowledged authority to certain limitations; but the compact that imposes these checks, and settles the conditions, betrays collusion with the foe, and is treason against God. True virtue and piety begin when all compromises with sin are at an end, and when the soul has pledged itself to unconditional obedience and devotion. Life begun and prosecuted under the sanction of so high a consecration, cannot prove a failure. Dark days may lower over its pathway. Sore struggles may be appointed as tests of sincerity, and for the discipline of those who aspire to do the bidding of God in a higher sphere, but for ultimate discomfiture there is no place in such a career. The spirit in which the enterprise is conceived is a pledge of success. Its lofty aims bring it into alliance with unfailing, Divine resources.

In passing on to apply some of the practical lessons suggested by this discussion, I shall transpose the order of its topics, and accept my first theme of exhortation from the conclusion of the argument.

"*Overcome the wicked one.*" Lay the foundation of success in all the moral and intellectual enterprises to which conscience and your own generous aspirations invite you in a decisive, unqualified, instantaneous renunciation of every bad or doubtful habit, and in a brave, unreserved, immediate, life-long devotion to every virtue and every duty to which you are held by any obligation, Divine or human. To young men, far more than to middle life or old age, is applicable that startling passage of Holy Scripture, "Behold, *now* is the accepted time; behold, *now* is the day of salvation." Genuine conversions are always sudden. Visible progress in virtue may be slow, and its beginning inappreciable; but the hour which witnesses the entrance of the new principle, and plants the germ of a new life, constitutes a well-defined era in the moral history of a man, as well as a memorable crisis in his moral character. The vacillations that precede, and the struggles that sometimes follow, the moment consecrated by high resolves and heavenly grace, may be remembered as parts of the same period of doubtfulness and darkness, but they are historically distinct, and lie on opposite sides of the great turning-point in character and destiny. Whoever would reform his life, and "turn from the power of Satan unto God," must begin by having faith in his own deliberate purpose, formed in the fear of the Lord, and in reliance upon heavenly grace. Such a purpose is the starting-place of every successful enterprise of virtue and improvement. Let the young man who aspires to become either virtuous or wise, take his position on this high vantage-ground. Let him inquire, if he has not brought with him thus far some unsatisfied convictions of duty, and purposes of reform and improvement which as yet have found no realization in the daily life? We need not admonish him that the tendency, the error, the sin, which now has but a feeble hold upon him, and will readily yield to the corrective force of virtuous resolution and manly effort, speedily makes for itself an impregnable stronghold in the inveteracy of habit, and is thus enabled to bid defiance to all ordinary reformatory endeavours. These incipient vices make haste to expand into prolific sources of evil, and to pour their polluting streams into the tide of life. It has long been with me an established opinion, that the majority of educated men pass through life shorn of half their strength for want of a symmetrical, well expressed mental and moral development. Hardly less considerable is the proportion of young men engaged in a career of education, who forfeit its chief benefits, and go forth unfurnished for the demands of life, just because they will not be at the pains of correcting petty faults before they become habits, and of forming a virtuous, manly, vigorous character, at the only time when such an achievement is possible. Some minds pertinaciously resist all attempts to ingraft more liberal ideas and elevated sentiments, more refined tastes and more graceful manners, upon their original stock. No skill or assiduity of the teacher is able even to eliminate the provincialisms and vulgarisms of their spoken and written language, to correct an unnatural tone, or reform an ungainly attitude or gesture. No friendly converse can lure them away from the deteriorating, vulgarizing associations and affinities to which they yield up body and soul, from the moment they cross the threshold of a place of education. A few weeks or a few months of vigilant self-inspection and yielding docility, of vigorous resolution and manly effort, are sufficient to correct such faults and supply such deficiencies, and to purify the literary neophyte from the grosser elements derived from careless training or unfortunate associations; but this is a price which he cannot be induced to offer for improvements indispensable alike to success and respectability in his chosen career.

I dwell the more at large upon this lower and less important aspect of a great practical evil, not only because I would make manifest the baleful tendency of an error into which many fall with little forethought of consequences, but because we have here a palpable and unsuspected illustration of its higher moral bearings. We readily condemn the folly of the reckless youth who resolves to carry with him into life all the bad tastes, and vulgar sentiments, and coarse manners, and low habits which he brought to college, as well as all that the worst associations of a college can impart to him. What shall we say, then, of him who, with equal levity, passes through this forming period, not of life only, but of being, disfigured with moral blemishes, and making no effort to deliver the soul from the vicious habitudes and hateful malformations that are to be the burden and dishonour of its entire existence? It is by temptations as feeble, and for indulgences as worthless, as any that ever blinded and enthralled the victim of indolence and degrading impulses, that many a thoughtful and high-minded young man consents to a forfeiture of all good hopes, and thwarts the great designs of Heaven's mercy in behalf of his soul. It is because he will not allow grave care to cloud the enjoyments and disturb the occupations of the present moment, that he goes on from year to year preferring dreams to realities. It is because he lacks the nerve to interfere with illusions which he knows can only deceive and ruin him, that he madly trifles with imperishable interests, and braves whatever there may be of danger in God's wrath, when provoked to the uttermost by a guilty man. Who can hope to break the spell by which "the wicked one" holds such a man in vile durance? Who to gain his audience for the sober lessons of truth? And yet he must pause and think—he must struggle and break his bands asunder—he *must* smite his enemy with a deadly stroke, or prepare for evils which an archangel's intellect cannot compute. This series of postponements must soon be exhausted, and that last hour come in which even prayer and a soul-struggle cannot be of any avail. Under such conditions, it is not like a man to shrink from this inevitable crisis. Young man, fear to plunge into life with life's great problem unsolved. You venture out upon a bottomless sea with a millstone hung about your neck. Subdue the enemy within your own bosom, and then may you go with a whole and a brave heart into the great conflict before you. You would be strong, valiant men, fit for worthy enterprises. Begin this great conflict of life by trampling Satan under your feet. Make alliances with God, and holy men, and good angels, and you shall win the field. To-day, if ye hear his voice—to-day, if you will be wise or strong, "harden not your heart."

II. *Let the word of God abide in you.* Treasure it up in your heart as an unspeakably precious deposit. God hath bestowed upon you no better gift. It is the expression of his own ineffable wisdom. He sent you into this world of trial a stranger and a pilgrim; and this is the infallible guide which he ordained for your safety and salvation. Follow it implicitly. Obey it reverently. Listen to the oracles Divine with profound, absolute devotion. To profess faith in the Bible as the veritable word of Jehovah, and, at the same time, to withhold obedience, involves a gross inconsistency peculiarly unworthy of a rational, intelligent man. Without dwelling further upon the moral aspects of such a delinquency, we commend a reverent and habitual recognition of the "word of God" as the source of mental power, and an incomparable auxiliary to great intellectual achievements. It has been said, most erroneously, by a great ethical writer, that when a course of right action has become habitual, it is no matter how soon the reasons for its adoption are forgotten. On the contrary, it is a radical defect in mere habitual virtue, that it speedily degenerates into dull, irksome routine, and gradually loses the vitality and earnestness which are essential to all high performance. For this paralyzing tendency there is in most constitutions no remedy but what may be supplied by the power and permanence of the actuating motive. So long as the mind is kept under the influence of strong and predominating considerations and interests, its energies are likely to be kept in full play, and neither habit nor old age can dry up the sources of its vigour and activity. We know of no mental habitude more favourable to the full development and lasting efficiency of the intellectual powers than that of keeping the soul in perpetual, conscious communion with its highest sources of activity. It is an inspiring, as well as a hallowing thought, that we are performing a part assigned to us by the Divine wisdom, and in accordance with God's own specific directions. Something of a Divine influence, we had almost said of the divinity itself, rests upon and pervades that mind which derives its maxims, and imbibes its spirit, from Heaven's living oracles. "Whosoever drinketh of this water shall never thirst—it shall be in him a well of water, springing up into everlasting life." Once enthroned as the supreme arbiter of human pursuits, the word of God is able completely to harmonize the soul's jarring, conflicting impulses, and to bring the emotional and moral nature of man into fraternal alliance and co-operation with the understanding. The sublime principles and sublimer hopes which it supplies become incorporated with a new life, of which every purpose, and plan, and effort, is instinct with a power more than human. The indwelling monitor, heeded thoughtfully and reverently obeyed, grows to be the source of all genial aspirations and joys, as well as of authority. Obedience to such a rule of life, begun early, and carried out in all of life's pursuits, consciously and cordially, inspires our entire earthly career with something like the buoyancy and freshness of perpetual youth. It supplies an antidote for distaste and discouragement—it supplies all needful resources against the day of defeat or disaster, by making God a partner and co-worker in all our enterprises. It is the only expedient known either to philosophy or experience for furnishing with an adequate supply of cheering, invigorating motive, the rapidly approaching period of sere and sapless old age. The young man in whom the word of God abideth and reigneth, has discovered the fabled herb which bids away the fell disease of age, and beautifies and refreshes the soul with perpetual youth. "He shall be like a tree planted by the rivers of water, that bringeth forth his fruit in his season; his leaf also shall not wither, and whatsoever he doeth shall prosper."

Finally. "*I have written unto you, young men, because ye are strong.*" Bodily and mental vigour belong to the young, as physical attributes. Their energies are fresh and unwasted. They plan courageously, and execute with a strong hand. These are spontaneous tendencies of youth, and they indicate very intelligibly the duties of this period, so important in the history of human life. "Rejoice, O young man, in thy youth, and let thy heart cheer thee in the days of thy youth." Be strong. "Whatsoever thy hand findeth to do, do it with thy might." Make the *most* of the powers intrusted to you. Cultivate the habit of *doing your best* in all your undertakings. Put your highest energies in requisition. Summon to your aid the strongest impulses which the enterprise in hand is entitled to enlist in its favour. You are a student. Strive to go to the bottom of every subject of investigation. Aim at nothing less than a thorough knowledge of every author and every branch of science to which you direct your attention, less for the scholarly acquisitions which it ensures, than for the mental habits it induces. Accustom yourself to superficial study and negligent investigation, and you soon become incapable of any other. The mind speedily learns the bad art of being satisfied with this degraded standard of performance, and of thinking well of its mean attainments. It ceases to know, or even to suspect, that there are depths beyond the measurements of its own short line, and in the very profoundness of its ignorance grows conceited, and egotistic, and flippant. Some years consumed in scholastic pursuits, conducted on such a plan, are likely to establish mental habits utterly incompatible with any masculine development or honourable achievement in after life, just as the prisoner, long confined to his cell, loses the power of vigorous and graceful locomotion, or as the invalid, bed-ridden for half a lifetime, never afterward aspires to do more than creep softly along covered piazzas and shady alcoves. On the contrary, earnest, vigorous intellectual effort soon becomes easier than any other, because it rallies the mind's best powers, and is sustained by its strongest impulses. Such occupation is always pleasant, because distastes and ignominious sloth fly from the presence of a manly, vigorous movement; and honourable success, which earnest, brave endeavour never fails to secure, is itself an independent source of interest and satisfaction perpetually renewed.

I would inculcate the same doctrine in regard to all of the occupations in which an educated young man is likely to engage. Never enter upon any pursuit or profession which you do not deem worthy of your attention; and when your career is once resolved upon, devote to it your undivided energies. Aim at the highest excellence. *Do your best.* Some departments of professional life present stronger incitements than others to this generous outlay of earnestness and endeavour. The urgent competition of the bar, and the fact that its efforts are usually made in the presence of learned judges and advocates, who would not fail to detect and expose empty pretensions, afford, perhaps, the best guarantee against indolence and superficial attainments—a guarantee, however, which has not been able to exclude from the forum a considerable number of incompetent men. The physician performs his functions in a more private sphere, and, for the most part, in the presence of unprofessional spectators, where it is more easy to make pretension and bluster pass for science. The danger of being content with superficial attainments, and of falling into habits of mental lethargy, is proportionably increased, and with it the need of moral incitements to a faithful and wise discharge of duties as important and sacred as any which do not more directly act upon the moral and intellectual interests of man.

It is worthy of especial observation, that those professions which are most intimately concerned with the highest interests of the race, are more than others remote from the operation of ordinary worldly motives, and to a greater extent left to the power of conscientious and religious considerations. This is eminently the case with teachers of youth, whose functions are never effectively performed without such a degree of professional enthusiasm, or of conscientious devotion to duty, as will supply the resources of strong impulses and unfailing earnestness. The man who has nothing to bring to these duties but so much work for so much pay—who retires satisfied when he has read his lecture, and made his criticisms, and recorded delinquencies, may be pronounced wholly unfit for the responsibilities of a profession which acts upon *mind.* He might become a respectable artisan or labourer, but not a teacher of youth. He is not fit to be trusted with the culture of intellect. He does not sympathize with its wants or destinies. Whoever rightly comprehends these will shrink from the responsibilities of the teacher's profession, or he will labour to satisfy them with all the solicitude that a sense of personal and religious obligation can inspire. He will habituate himself to reflect that he is engaged in making impressions that must remain ineffaceable and immortal—that he is giving to mind such developments and tendencies as it shall bear with it through eternity—that no other man can correct his mistakes, or supply his deficiencies, or atone for his faults. What he does, must remain forever essentially unchanged; what he neglects to do, will remain undone. Even professional enthusiasm, without this higher sense of the moral relations of his calling, will prove an insufficient incitement to fidelity to the claims of duty. It may ensure all due attention to pupils of quick parts and aspiring minds, but this is precisely the class which has least occasion for the teacher's aid. The less gifted, the tardier mind, the timid, the thoughtless, and even the indolent youth, has claims upon the teacher not less sacred; and the untiring zeal, and patient, conscientious fidelity with which he applies himself to the self-denying work of developing *such* minds, in so far as they are susceptible of improvement, and of *doing his best* with every individual committed to his instruction, constitutes the highest test of excellency in his vocation. Whoever is above or below this toilsome detail—whoever does not think *any sane mind,* made immortal by its God, worthy to engage his solicitude and his labours—has no special calling to the work of a teacher. He may win a reputation by his success with apt, ambitious pupils; but his negligence, impatience, contempt for others, who are also to be trained for eternity, intellectually as well as morally, and the scantiness of whose resources the more urgently demands a painstaking culture, are offences against humanity and morality, which it would not be easy to characterize by epithets too strong. I dwell the more earnestly upon this topic, because a very considerable proportion of our graduates engage either for a season or permanently in the business of teaching, and I would inspire them with a deep sense of the responsibilities they perhaps too inconsiderately assume. I would encourage them to enter upon this work with enlarged views and the most Christian purposes. It ranks next to the Christian ministry in its intimate relations with man's highest interests, and in the dignity of the greatest usefulness. More properly, it is itself a Christian ministry, co-operating with the Gospel in exalting the human family to intelligence and purity, and in fitting men for the joys and occupations of heaven. Lower views than these of the teacher's function will prove too feeble to sustain his vigour and fidelity under the trials and distastes incident to his vocation, and to resist the temptations to discouragement and relaxed effort, which perverseness, indolence, and inaptitude will never fail to supply; while the consciousness of toiling, not with the low ambition of qualifying a few more gifted pupils to acquire distinction in literary or professional life, but with the holy purpose of preparing *all*, according to the measure of mental capacity bestowed upon them by the Creator, for the destinies of their endless being, is likely to prove an unfailing source of encouragement and strenuous activity.

In conclusion, I apply the teachings of this discussion to the Christian ministry. All who aspire to this holy function, our argument admonishes to come to its toils prepared to put forth the highest mental and moral energies with which nature, study, and the grace of God have endowed them. Here, more than in any secular pursuit, success is proportioned to the spirit of consecration and self-sacrifice in which the work is done, rather than to the measure of native or acquired endowments. Such a spirit, however, supposes the most earnest endeavours to acquire qualifications for usefulness no less than earnestness in the use of them. It breathes itself forth in the preparations of the closet no less than in the efforts of the pulpit. God has joined these things together, and the man who presumptuously puts them asunder does it at the certain peril of his usefulness, no less than of his reputation. That Divine grace which, beyond all controversy, is the great element of saving power, does, with great uniformity, co-operate with the clearest, strongest, and most earnest inculcation of truth ; while the preacher whose thoughts are feeble, puny, and obscure, and uttered heartlessly, is never likely to be honoured with a sanction which might be mistaken for Heaven's approbation of ignorance or indolence. The Church has never more reason to be ashamed than of ministers who no longer *try to preach well*—who only go to their study to read newspapers and periodicals, and have nothing fresher and better for their pulpit than the dry, cold fragments of oft-tasted feasts, or the yet more refuse and unwholesome viands which the troublous agitations of the moment are able to galvanize into some of the lower forms of life. It is wonderful that the least spark of piety should not deter men from bringing such *cheap* offerings before God. And yet one often hears such moral enormities justified and defended on something like logical and Christian grounds. The minister should not be forever pressing upon his highest notes. He should guard against the danger of exciting expectations which he will not be able, without much inconvenience, to satisfy. It is not quite compatible with humility to labour so incessantly after uncommon thoughts and classical expressions. The minister must *come down* to the common mind if he would not lose the sympathies of his audience. The most common argument of all—it betrays an overweening confidence in human effort, and too little sense of dependence upon God, to lay so much stress upon great sermons. These truisms must all essentially fail of sheltering laziness and folly under their philosophic or saintly garb, since, in so far as they are of any application to the subject, they are embraced by the rule which ever demands at the preacher's hands the *best effort* he is able to make. It is great folly, as well as great arrogance, to talk of *coming down* to the popular mind. The sort of slip-shod, meaningless preaching to which I have adverted, is beyond all other human performances, incomprehensible by a popular assembly which grasps with ease and spontaneous intuition the luminous thoughts, and terse, clear argumentation and analysis of a really intelligent, earnest man. There is contagion in the movement of his spirit, and the hearer drinks in the deep import of his words without a tithe of the labour it costs to sift the eddying chaff of an empty, unimpassioned mind. The objection with which we are dealing takes it for granted that a sermon, which is the product of thoughtful, studious hours, must be dark with tantalizing metaphysics, or with turbulent scholastic or transcendental jargon, as if the man who thinks most vigorously, and prepares most carefully and systematically, were not more likely on that account to speak intelligibly. The theory suggested by our subject, as well as by every rational view of the Christian ministry, is not over-solicitous about the production of great, or learned, or highly-finished, or eloquent sermons; but it does imperatively demand that every preacher of the Gospel should put forth his utmost energies both for preparation and for performance—that he keep his soul all alive to the sacredness and fearful responsibilities of his calling—that he shun as a fatal, damnable dereliction, a negligent, perfunctory ministry, which satisfies itself with decent, easy routine, and deems it no offence to bring into the Divine presence a maimed sacrifice, that costs neither study nor prayer, and conciliates the favour of neither God nor man. So far as results are concerned, the measure of capacity or learning is of infinitely less importance than the spirit in which the work is done. God does unquestionably employ in his vineyard a great variety of talents and attainments, and he honours every man according to the fidelity and spirit of consecration with which he fulfils his mission; but there is no place for the idle—none for those who are only half awake—none for those who are not prepared to "make full proof of their ministry," who are not of a fervent spirit, ready to endure hardness, or bonds, or death, for Christ's sake.

It is a source of unspeakable satisfaction, that, in defiance of ever-multiplying temptations to worldliness and ambition, so many of the students and graduates of this University are devoted in purpose to this sacred calling. Let them be entreated to remember well that the Christian ministry is not a work for drones. "Be ye strong." "Quit you like men." Make your sacrifices in a liberal, magnanimous spirit. Hold no base parleying with flesh and blood. Ask of the Crucified, "Lord, what wilt thou have me to do?" and let the responsive oracle be henceforth the law of your being. O rejoice to lay your talents, and your scholarship, and your life at the foot of the cross! "I write unto you, young men, because ye are strong." By the grace of God you can achieve something worth living for. Be ever mindful of what Divine resources are at the command of your prayer of faith. Seize upon them all, and consecrate them all to the service of Him "who hath loved you, and given himself for you." Shun no labour —no sacrifices. Give the best of your life, of your learning, of your genius, and your eloquence, if you possess them, to Him from whom you have received much more than all of these. You will be enriched by what you give. You will be made strong by the efforts you shall put forth. Such a consecration opens the way to the only true distinction. The only ambition worthy of a Christian scholar here finds its appropriate field of display.

THE END.

RESOURCES AND DUTIES

OF

CHRISTIAN YOUNG MEN.

A DISCOURSE TO THE

GRADUATING CLASS OF WESLEYAN UNIVERSITY,

AUGUST, 1845.

BY STEPHEN OLIN, D. D.

GEORGE PECK, EDITOR.

New-York:
PUBLISHED BY CARLTON & PHILLIPS,
200 MULBERRY-STREET.
1852.

RESOURCES AND DUTIES

OF

CHRISTIAN YOUNG MEN.

"Put ye on the Lord Jesus Christ, and make not provision for the flesh, to fulfill the lusts thereof."

ROMANS XIII, 14.

THIS text is highly figurative, but its intention and import are very obvious. It is an exhortation to be evangelically and thoroughly religious. The first eleven chapters of the Epistle to the Romans are devoted to the exposition and inculcation of Christian doctrines. The twelfth and thirteenth are hortatory and preceptive. They announce our practical duties, and warn of dangers to be shunned. They declare, with authority and without any reserve at all, that we are held, under the gospel dispensation, to the highest style of virtue, both in the motive and in the performance. As far as concerns the principle of our movements in the new life, "love is the fulfilling of the law," while in point of fact and actual manifestation, believers are called upon to "present their bodies a living sacrifice, holy and acceptable unto God, which is their reasonable service," to "prove what is that good, and acceptable, and perfect will of God." Our text announces the true method of attaining these vital Christian objects in reference both to the motive and the manifestation: "Put ye on the Lord Jesus Christ, and make not provision for the flesh, to fulfill the lusts thereof."

There is a numerous and very interesting class of persons entitled to our respect by their intelligence and moral worth, and appealing strongly to our sympathies by the false and highly critical position which they occupy. They are undoubting believers in the Christian religion, and warm, avowed admirers of its sublime theology, pure ethics, and divine philanthropy. Yet they are not Christians. They are destitute not only of the hopes, but also of the secure any, even the smallest of the spiritual advantages which the gospel offers, by stealth. God, and our own moral nature, call for open, manly confession, and both will assuredly disown and denounce all pretensions to piety which shun exposure to the broad light of the day. Nothing can be effectually done in this work till the sincere aspirant after Christian excellence fairly assumes his position, and becomes, as he is intended to be, "a spectacle to men and to angels"—"a city set on a hill that cannot be hid." We not only have lessons to learn for our own improvement, but lessons to exemplify for the improvement of others and for the Saviour's honor. They only who run lawfully win the prize, and none others are likely to receive the precious aids indispensable to success. This we might expect from all we know of ourselves or of God's attributes, and of this we are notified in his word. Till a man assumes an avowed and recognized Christian position, he has no full scope for the exercise of his own proper resources, and no adequate occasions for calling up his powers. The state of indecision and divided aspirations which precedes the final and formal decision of this great question, is little better than a paralysis of the soul. There is seldom any distinct vision, and never any earnest, well-directed purpose or action, until this moral crisis is passed. But with the assumption of his true Christian position, at the moment of "putting on the Lord Jesus Christ;" not on religious, supernatural grounds alone, but on philosophical also, the man receives an investiture of high powers and immunities. It is an important point gained to have it known to which party we belong. The sight of the banner that floats over our heads will not fail of clearing away many annoyances and many enemies, and of bringing to our aid troops of powerful auxiliaries. The courage of the soldier rises with the putting on of his uniform, and still more at sight of the marshaled hosts that throng the outspread field.

The responsibilities of a Christian profession, so often feared and shunned as and neglect. Better tastes, too, are cultivated; so that what were seductive pleasures, and so powerful temptations once, lose their character and become an offense. Walking by faith, the Christian appreciates more and more completely the excellence of the heavenly objects with which he is thus made familiar, and so acquires a standard of comparison which he can but be ever applying to the worldly objects and enjoyments that invite his regards. Such a process cannot fail to wean him from perishable good, and so leave him more free from every weight.

While this Christian process strengthens perpetually the motives and the aids to piety, and abates the force of opposition, it has a yet stronger tendency to improve the *quality* of our virtues. Nothing is more likely to retard and discourage a generous mind, intent on the attainment of the highest excellence, than a perpetual consciousness, or even suspicion, that its best performances are marred by the admixture of some base alloy; that some low, selfish motive may have been active, though unperceived, in the production of its most shining deeds. We may acquire humility or modesty from worldly disappointments and mortifications, but some measure of misanthropy and discontent are likely to be derived from the same lessons. It is not always easy to practice beneficence and charity, to exert the highest public, or social, or private virtues, without having, whether we will or not, some reference to the returns which we are likely to receive in the form of gratitude, or reputation, or public confidence, or posthumous fame. This selfishness, to whatever extent it mingles with our motives, not only produces a sense of self-degradation, but it is, in fact, degrading to our performances and character; and so largely does this debasing alloy enter into our spirit and conduct, and so utterly impossible is it to exclude it altogether, without some more potent exorcism than mere human virtue can summon to its assistance, that most men, after some vain struggles against its occult, malignant influence, yield to its dominion, and become satisfied with doing their duty, without much concern about the motive. Under such circumstances it is but too obvious that virtue has nothing left besides its form and its name. It has no longer any power to purify, etherealize, and exalt our nature. It is a mere earthly thing, a matter of business, a balancing of interests and conveniences, a skillful and comprehensive solution of the question, How can we take the best care of ourselves? I am quite sure that many will find, in their own consciousness and recollections, manifold illustrations of the evil I have exposed. Now he who has "put on the Lord Jesus Christ," has found a perfect antidote for this evil. He has become a disciple, that he may be saved; and he devotes his entire life to Christ, who was crucified for him, as a matter of gratitude and pious obligation. "Love is the perfecting of the law," and this is a motive from which self is wholly excluded. We work, we suffer, we live for another, even for Him who died for us, and rose again. When we have fully "put on Christ," then is love made perfect, and all fear and all selfishness is fully "cast out." Disenthralled from all low, personal ends, and seeking only how we may please Christ, we enter upon a high, holy career of virtue, which can never know the taint of worldly maxims, which finds its model, its resources, and its ends, in Jesus Christ, our Lord. Gratitude, love, loyalty, these are the motives by which all heaven is swayed. They impel the angels onward in their career, and yet more the "spirits of just men made perfect." Indeed, heavenly pursuits, and enjoyments, and virtues, are no other than those into which the good man is introduced when he "puts on Christ,"—the remote and invisible parts of the orbit in which he has already begun to move.

As the Christian motive is the only one which can be trusted for purity, so it is the only one that can be relied on for efficiency. "Love is stronger than death." A man will often do for the love of his friend, or his family, what he could not do on any lower impulse. But if affection for kindred, according to the flesh, is able to minister strong impulses to the spirit, the love of Christ "*constrains* us." It imparts an energy something more than human, and qualifies for achievements only less than divine. A man's performances are likely to bear some proportion to the strength of the motives on which he acts. Now the great Christian motive, love to Christ, partakes of the superhuman and the godlike. It has the additional advantage of stability. It cannot be impaired by time, or change, or circumstance, but attains dominion over the soul, potent in exact proportion to our progress in piety. The racer moves more swiftly as he approaches the goal. A body tending to the earth, gains speed in its descent. So the Christian is borne on with an ever accumulating momentum as he draws nearer to perfection in faith and love. When we add that Christ has provided divine assistance for all exigencies to which our human resources are unequal; that he gives the Holy Spirit to help our infirmities—to assure our hopes, illuminate our minds, and purify our hearts—I am unable to perceive what is yet wanting to a most admirable and all-sufficient apparatus of motives and means for the attainment of the highest moral excellence, and to the most glorious consummation of all that our fallen, but redeemed nature can aspire to.

I have already intimated—indeed, the text directly affirms, and this is its burden—that these great facilities for the prosecution of our moral improvement are suspended on the one condition of a sincere and hearty adoption of the gospel. We are "to put on the Lord Jesus Christ." He must become to us wisdom, and righteousness, and sanctification, and redemption—must be teacher, and priest, and only potentate. We must wear his livery, must go our warfare at his charges, and under his banner. Our dignity, our defense, and our exceeding great reward, must be sought and found in him. But we are not only called upon to make this entire dedication to Christ; we are also cautioned against all reservations: "Make not provision for the flesh, to fulfill the lusts thereof." Faith in Christ, and a resort to the gospel for pardon, and purity, and eternal life, presuppose an unconditional submission to its terms. Not one successful step can be taken in religion previously to the settlement of this grand preliminary. The mind may not be able at the outset to take in all the particulars involved in this great act of submission, but it can and does embrace them implicitly; and it is of the very essence of all right faith to confide in Christ to the uttermost, and to consent to follow him whithersoever he goeth, giving to the winds all anxiety about the special paths in which we may be called to proceed in our onward march to heaven. Christ's dignity and sovereignty are concerned in imposing such conditions as he pleases, and in receiving no terms at the hand of the sinner; and he will unquestionably use his disciples in just such services, and impose upon them just such burdens, as he sees best, giving no pledges in advance, but the assurance that his grace shall be sufficient for them. I know well that a multitude, even of professing

Christians, begin and prosecute what is called a religious course, on a very different plan. They give law to religion. They retain as many indulgences, and concede as many sacrifices, as may fall in with their tastes. They make provision for pride, and ambition, and sensuality, and self-will, and "put on the Lord Jesus Christ" only in so far as they think he may set off their own purple and fine linen to the best advantage. But my business to-day is with the sincere, who wish to be made holy and to be saved by Christ, and who really desire to know the conditions of success. I take it upon me to warn all such to beware of admitting *any worldly, or selfish motive, or consideration whatever,* into the settlement of this great question between God and their souls. I take it upon me to proclaim that all such tampering in the business of religion will certainly prove fatal to any well-founded hopes of success in the Christian career. Whoever stops to inquire whether it may cost him sacrifices to be a Christian, with any intention to hesitate if it does, has admitted a consideration utterly incompatible with his becoming a Christian at all. Whoever chooses his creed or his church with any, the slightest, reference to the honor, or the ease, or the emolument, it may give or withhold, does, by such an admission, utterly vitiate all his claim to have any part or lot in the matter of saving piety. I do not speak of those who knowingly and deliberately make these their chief grounds of preference; but I affirm that it is wholly antichristian, and an insult to the crucified Saviour, to yield any, the smallest, place to worldly motives in choosing the Christian position which we will occupy. Let Christ and conscience decide in this matter. "Put ye on the Lord Jesus Christ, and make not provision for the flesh, to fulfill the lusts thereof." The gospel will admit of no compromise here. This is its point of honor, which it cannot, and will not, yield by a single iota. I feel called upon to use the language of unmeasured denunciation against a mistake, so often fatal to hopeful beginnings in religion; so very often fatal to the religious prospects of young men.

I deem this point of sufficient importance to receive more particular and detailed illustration.

Without stopping here to consider the grosser forms which this grave offense against the Saviour's dignity familiarly assumes, I will only refer to such as are most likely to be found in cultivated, aspiring minds. A demand is often put forth in this quarter for more tasteful developments of Christianity than we are wont to meet with in its every-day history. Accustomed to look for the beautiful and the poetical in their speculations as well as in external objects, persons of this class can conceive of nothing higher or nobler in the gospel than its adaptations to minister to this universal want of cultivated, polished society; and they have little true respect, and less sympathy, for any manifestation of piety which does not conform to their special tastes. They have a theory on the subject, which requires that the divine Author of all the beauty and harmony of the material world, as well as the world of intellect, should, for still higher reasons, observe the same great principles in his plans and operations for bringing men to heaven. I have stated the substance of the theory, which is, however, variously modified by habit, education, and temperament. And I remark that this demand upon the gospel quite loses sight of the fact, that the salvation of souls is its grand design and object, to which mental and social improvement are only incidental and secondary; that Christianity finds the world immersed in darkness, and vice, and depravity; so that its great work on earth is that of elaboration, of renovation, of preparation, for a higher estate of mature graces and perfect harmonies. It has, of necessity, a great deal of rough work to do; its processes must be adapted to the material to be acted on, no less than to the results to be produced. The symphonies divine that charm the angels are not so well fitted to this sinful world, which has contrived to array its tempers, and tastes, and tendencies, against its Maker, in a hostility far more brutish than angelic.

The means and appliances of the gospel, in order to be effective, must recognize the conditions and the disabilities of the beings over whom its conquests are to be won; and whoever would be an effective co-worker with God in this broad field, must, like God, be content to accommodate his message and ministry to the multitude. Let no man who has raised himself to the great purpose of living for his race and for eternity, indulge in the idle fancy that he can gain his chosen end by herding with the philosophers, and propounding Christianity to the multitude in learned theses. Let him rather come down from the high places of intellectual pride, and put himself in communication with the masses. These are not yet polished, or intelligent, or able to appreciate all that in heaven will be familiar as household words. In the most favorable state of society which has ever existed on the earth, the multitude of men have been uneducated—have been doomed to toil, and to comparative poverty. To this condition of our race the gospel at first adapted its lessons and its agencies, it may be, from choice, but assuredly from necessity—a necessity that still exists in all its force. I may add, that the demand for more tasteful or philosophical developments of Christianity can only be satisfied at the expense of the immensely important class of men for whose special benefit the Christian revelation was promulgated—for "the gospel was preached to the poor." The reform proposed might accommodate the tenth of a tithe of the population of highly civilized nations; but its natural tendency would be to separate this favored class from the masses, and bring them under a Christian culture, the most intellectual and graceful it may be, but wholly inapplicable to the condition and wants of the people. These, forsaken by their natural guides, their candlesticks removed from their midst, must sink into hopeless impiety and ignorance but for God's mercy, which is wont to interpose, and raise up prophets from among themselves.

But this divine interference for the prevention of results, utterly and eternally ruinous, does not adequately provide against some of the most deplorable evils that mar the piety, and fetter the energies, of the church. The gospel is a leveler, and contemplates our whole sinful race as "made of one blood." It will have "the rich and the poor meet together" at the feet of Jesus, and forget all earthly distinctions in rapt meditation on the infinite goodness and glory of God, and on the heavenly world, to which they both look by faith, as to a common inheritance. It will have the lettered and the untaught, the high-born and the low, mingle before a common altar, and bow down before a common Saviour. It abhors caste, and is ambitious of bringing together in one vast brotherhood of faith, and feeling, and co-operation, all blood-bought souls. It will have the rich contribute their wealth, the noble their influence, the learned their wisdom, the poor their sterling virtues, their patient toil, their might of sympathy and of sinew, to the building up of a pure and powerful church. It is by the combination of all classes, and all talents, that human society prospers most, and, for aught that appears, it is the Saviour's design to constitute and edify the church upon the same principle. Now the pride of man comes in to thwart this benevolent design. It will have an aristocracy, where Heaven can, least of all, tolerate it. It puts asunder what God has joined together. As far as the antichristian theory, against which I so earnestly protest, is carried out in practice, it monopolizes and covers up the light. It sequesters talent and influence but to place them in positions where they act not at all, or at the greatest disadvantage, upon the general interests of religion and humanity.

Nor must I pass over, as too unimportant to deserve notice, the inevitable tendency of this religious exclusiveness to generate a spirit and a power antagonist to the universal equality guarantied by our free institutions. We have no privileged orders, nor is it likely, in the existing temper of the public mind, that talent, or wealth, or ancestry, or even great virtues, will ever give to their possessors a social position dangerous to the rights of the humblest citizen; but I must think the lovers of our republican institutions and manners will have some cause for solicitude, if the growing tendency among our influential classes to desert the popular walks of religion, for more select and pretending connections, shall increase in a similar ratio for twenty or fifty years to come. The danger is not at all diminished by Christian forms and names; and a religious aristocracy which is completely sheltered under the guaranties of universal freedom of conscience, secured to all by our free institutions, has no security to give in return to those institutions, that it will not at least generate a spirit dangerous to their purity and perpetuity. No pride is more blinding and corrupting than spiritual pride, and men who are ever fancying themselves upon a lofty eminence, unconsciously acquire a habit of looking *down* upon the rest of the world.*

A question of far deeper import is this: What are the more strictly religious effects

* See Note A, at the end.

of this defection from the popular Christianity upon the persons most concerned? How is it with the dainty seceders who loathe the manna that "covers the face of the wilderness," of which "every man may gather according to his eating," and deem it distasteful to receive with the multitude, seated on the ground, the bread which Jesus so liberally blesses and breaks? Of all who lightly turn away from the lowlier faith of their early education and their fathers' house, to rear their showy altars upon the high places of the land, whether seduced by vanity, or ambition, or fastidiousness, it may well be doubted if many secure more than the shadow of true religion. If they have borne with them to this false, exposed position, some measure of spirituality, the growth of a more fruitful soil, and of a more benignant clime, it speedily withers and decays for want of a participation in those popular sympathies, from which they start back with a disgust so profound. Their dwelling places are unquestionably on the Parnassus or the Olympus of the Christian world, but these mountain tops have neither depth of earth, nor springs of water, and no plant of righteousness is likely to strike its roots into the hard rock that composes their shining but arid summits.

Such aristocratic aspirants after a graceful piety, (I call them aristocratic for want of a better term to mark this perverse development of Christianity,) naturally fall into two classes, and exhibit two great corruptions of the gospel. The more intellectual and philosophical part commonly wander into that cold region of unfruitful speculations, where rationalism or transcendentalism, or whatever neology happens to be in fashion, claims empire. The merely fashionable, and ambitious, and fastidious portion, more usually pay their courtly homage to graceful forms or venerable reminiscences, and find and exhibit, at least, some of the semblances of spiritual piety in the religion of the imagination.*

I cannot part with the topic under consideration without bestowing a passing thought upon the God-dishonoring senti-

* See Note B, at the end.

ments in which this deplorable fallacy has its origin. This demand for a Christianity more refined and tasteful than that of Christ, proceeds upon the assumption that God is specially pleased and honored by the conversion of persons of literary taste, and polished manners; of men accustomed to good society, and well read in good authors. Disguise it as we will, that is the fundamental idea of this antichristian theory. Now, for aught that appears, these accomplishments do not figure very largely in Heaven's estimate of man. I cannot help suspecting that John Bunyan, John Nelson, and worthies of this class, wore, in God's sight, the insignia of a truer and higher nobility, than the choicest spirits of the brilliant eras of Elizabeth and Anne.

What are the attributes most prized and most sought for in man, by the crucified Saviour? Charity and purity. These are the cardinal virtues of the gospel. Every one that loveth is born of God, and knoweth God. If we love one another, God dwelleth in us, and his love is perfected in us. God is love, and he that dwelleth in love, dwelleth in God, and God in him. The entire law is fulfilled by him who loves God with all the heart, and his neighbor as himself. This is glory to God in the highest, peace on earth, and good will to men. The gospel is satisfied when this great end is achieved, and it labors, from age to age, to implant this law of universal affinity and brotherhood in all hearts, and thus to establish a vast system of order and divine harmony, worthy of the wisdom and of the mercy of God. And this is its primary, proper object. High intellectual culture, advanced civilization, refinement of sentiments and of manners, do indeed attend, or rather follow, its progress, but only as incidental results of the great moral changes which have their sphere in the moral nature and character of man. The moral transformation is all that the gospel, as such, aims to accomplish. This makes the sinner a child of God, fits him for heavenly society and pursuits, makes him a joint heir with Christ. These are no doubtful announcements, but first principles of the gospel, which no sane Christian will for a moment call in question; and they suggest the irresistible conclusion, that that is the most Christian church, and that the most apostolic ministry, which most successfully accomplish these most Christian ends. No matter who they are that are converted, and sanctified, and brought to heaven. The ignorant, the outcast, the Hottentot, the slave—these are Christ's well-beloved brethren, and with him heirs of God. The princes of this world may be glad to go to heaven, if they may, in such company, and angels would exult to be co-workers with God in preaching the gospel to the poor. What lesson of instruction do I find in this digression? A stern rebuke of that wretched fastidiousness which refuses to be satisfied with such a type of Christianity as satisfies Christ—demonstrative proof that this reiterated demand for a more tasteful and philosophical religion is unreasonable and unphilosophical, as well as unchristian—new force in the exhortation, "Make not provision for the flesh, to fulfill the lusts thereof." Would you find for yourselves a religion adapted to the soul's pressing wants, and to the demands of a perishing world? Drink deeply of the Christian sentiments and sympathies of the people. Would you act a heroic part in the holy war which God and good men are carrying on against error and sin? Throw yourselves into the midst of the masses, where there are most hearts to be won, and most souls to be saved. Do not be for ever gazing at the toy that glitters on the top of the steeple, but bend your regards upon the living stones that compose Christ's holy temple, upon the undying souls that throng its inner and outer courts. There the true altar and the authorized priest are sure to be found, and there God has work to do for all, who, like his well-beloved Son, are content to abase themselves, that they may be exalted.

I have not left time for the discussion of some other topics which I cannot wholly overlook. Educated young men often find another stumbling block in the presumed or dreaded interference of an honest consecration to Christ with their ambitious, and, as they are prone to esteem them, their pure and honorable aspirations. My own observations on this subject would lead me to regard this as one of the most common and fatal causes of backsliding, as well as procrastination. Many, who hear and recognize the voice of God, refuse to enter his vineyard, because they are not quite sure that the employments and immunities to be assigned them there will be agreeable and satisfactory. Impiety never assumes a more daring attitude than this, however the rank offense may be disguised or concealed by circumstances or by false reasonings. What is implied by the postponement or abandonment of a religious course on such grounds? Distrust in God is implied, and unbelief in its most odious, atrocious, insolent form. Has God, then, no *right* to interfere with our plans? This mental discipline, and these accomplishments, which are too good to be subjected to his control—were they acquired—are they held, on terms altogether independent of Jehovah? Is the inexperienced youth, fresh from the schools and proverbially ignorant of the world, and of the future, somewhat better qualified to choose his own way, and thread the labyrinth of life alone, than God is to guide him? You will not be a Christian, because that confessedly assigns you a sphere of action where God and conscience must be consulted. You seek a freer range and a wider sphere. Take them, and then inquire if you are beyond the domain of God. Are you really freer to choose or surer to win? Is responsibility excluded, or danger of disappointment and disaster? No; for God reigns everywhere. All that is gained by this daring revolt against his authority is the dire privilege of working out our destiny without any promise of guidance, or grace, or reward, yet always under the divine supervision and control—always in conflict with his revealed will—always obnoxious to his displeasure, and certain of ultimate ruin whatever fortunes may be conceded to a career which is, at best, only a prolonged rebellion against God.

After saying so much of the religious aspects of this case, I must not omit to expose the shallow views of life on which this great practical error is based. As a class, truly pious men are the most fortunate in the world. Estimate their successes by honors won, by their usefulness, by their attainments, or by their enjoyments, and these persons greatly outstrip their competitors. I will not stop to inquire why it is so, though I doubt not there is in the thing both a divine providence and a divine philosophy. Heaven guides and cheers on the man who is content to receive his commission from above, while the virtues and safeguards of religion do naturally minister to his successes even in secular pursuits. The fact, however, is all I contend for here. Common experience is a demonstration that godliness is profitable for this life, as well as that to come. It is something more than impiety—it is gross, blind folly, for a young man, setting out in life, to guard against the disturbing influence of religion in the settlement of his plans. God is likely to be his wisest counselor, and his most powerful auxiliary, and to exalt him in proportion to the humility of his submission to the divine authority.

I must add another remark. It is unquestionably true that piety often promotes, while it seldom retards, a man's progress in the world. It is no less so, and no less proper to mark the fact, that men who seek to make of religious pretensions, and church relations, instruments of ambition or gain, are almost sure of meeting with signal disappointment. Success in such attempts would offer a dangerous temptation to human virtue, and fill the churches with hypocrites; but success in such attempts, in such a country as this, where the government is neutral, and all sects have fair play, is nearly impossible. Aristocracy in religion meets with a potent antagonist in the legal and social democracy that universally prevails. Proscription for religious opinions is nearly impracticable in any form, where there is a multitude of sects, and the weak are prone to unite against any encroachment by the strong. In such a state of things there is an open field for industry and merit, in which no sectarian badge can win or lose the prize. There is no reward for the hypocrisy which would profess, or the base cowardice, or heartless prudence, which would shun to profess, any opinion or bear any name, for selfish objects. The temptation to sin in this matter is really so weak that there is little need of providing any safeguard against it, beyond a statement such as has been made. Neither cupidity nor vanity has much to gain by "making provision for the flesh," when neither emolument nor influence are to be won by recreancy to principle.

The short-sighted ambition which covets higher and brighter spheres of effort and manifestation than comport with the claims of duty, or the arrangements of Providence, is wont to fall into another capital error. In paying to circumstances their vain court for facilities and rewards, seldom granted but as the fruit of patient labor and practical self-denial, these impatient aspirants after distinction are insensibly led away from the only theatre of action adapted to their character and attainments. Talent is ever best developed, and commonly best rewarded, where it is most wanted.

It should therefore respect the great laws of demand and supply; and while the wide earth and boundless sea are open to its enterprise, should never press too eagerly into petty, glutted marts. An educated Christian young man, who, in all the attainable good before him, has eyes to see something better and nobler than mere pecuniary gain, cannot fail to perceive a most hopeful field of usefulness in his connection with one of the great popular Christian denominations of this country. It is unavoidable, that among the vast multitudes, so rapidly gathered into these broad folds by primitive zeal and labors, many will lack culture, and intelligence, and refinement. Education and literature, polished eloquence, and profound learning, naturally follow, though they seldom precede, the greatest successes of young and rising sects. When such wants are most pressing, precisely then is there likely to exist the most urgent demand for such qualifications to satisfy them.

A religious community whose successes have outstripped all its anticipations, suddenly finds itself responsible for the intellectual, as well as moral, improvement of millions. It has reached a point in its history where a demand for cultivated talent is of the most urgent character. It must have educated men; and literary attainment, when united with piety and good sense, is sure to be placed in positions the most favorable for the efficient exertion of extensive and salutary influence. It almost necessarily happens that learning, and eloquence, and refinement, acquire a consideration and a power to do good, great in proportion to their scarcity, and to the multitude of demands upon such qualifications. Just such a theatre as enlightened, sanctified ambition should most desire, is here opened to the Christian youth. It proffers useful, congenial, and honorable employment. It insures the earliest, fullest development of his mental and moral resources. It promises all reasonable and desirable exemption from the tedious probation and discouraging competition which he may be doomed to encounter elsewhere. It offers him equal and honorable partnership in the holy work of training a host of immortal beings for usefulness, purity, happiness, and heaven. The folly of turning away from these outspread fields waving with golden harvests, and echoing all around with Macedonian cries for more laborers, is only less than the guilt which is always superadded, when, in addition to this contempt for the suggestions of a sound discretion, some violence is also inflicted upon the conscience. And here I cannot refrain from a passing remark on the benignant relations which religion ever sustains to the practical movements of business and of life. So nicely and so graciously is the great scheme of an overruling, watchful providence, adapted to our various circumstances, that the most inexperienced youth —the merest novice in affairs—has little more to do, than simply to obey the dictates of an enlightened conscience, in order to secure all the advantages of the most comprehensive and well-digested plans, and of the deepest insight into the future. An unwavering trust in God and his word is the best guide, as well as the best safeguard. It is a great simplifier of life's complicated pursuits, and endows each single-hearted follower of Jesus Christ with a precocious, heavenly wisdom.

In anything I have said, I do not mean to intimate that both our actual piety and our Christian profession may not involve the most serious consequences. I know too well the genius of the gospel, to inculcate a doctrine so foreign from its avowals and its spirit. Great sufferings and great sacrifices do, unquestionably, enter into God's entire scheme for diffusing and propagating the true religion, and for the moral discipline of individuals. Christ was made perfect by suffering, and through much tribulation we are called to enter into the kingdom of heaven. Afflictions work out for the saints an exceeding weight of glory. Not only are Christians subject to the common lot of mortals, which is usually one of many pains and sorrows, but they are often called to suffer for Christ's sake. It is fundamental to the Christian system that men were redeemed by suffering, and hardly less so, as far as history is our teacher, that the best achievements of the gospel are to be carried in the midst of peril, and loss, and agony. In this great work of toil and sacrifice, it is no doubt the will of God that young men, and educated young men, shall have a principal share. God chooses them because they are strong, and he intends to make them the chief of his instruments for the accomplishment of his great designs of mercy. Let them look their calling fairly in the face, and enter on the career of duty, well aware of the conditions upon which they serve a crucified Redeemer. None more need to stir up the gift that is within them, to gird about their loins, and put on the armor of righteousness. I may safely say that no policy is so dangerous as caution and cowardice. I may confidently warn them of the folly and danger of "making provision for the flesh," by refraining from such a dedication as may exact from them the sternest conditions known to our Christian vocation. If great results can be attained by great efforts and great sufferings, what generous heart will refuse the sacrifice? If our own holiness and the happiness of others may be promoted in proportion to the expenditure of toil, or talent, or wealth, who will not feel that the outlay is reasonable and even politic? But the argument likely to be most effectual with ingenuous and truly pious minds is derived from the genius of our religion. The gospel is a way of salvation by grace. It lays the Christian under obligations immeasurably strong, which he can never satisfy, while it awakens in him a sense of gratitude ever restless and studious of methods by which it may testify its loyalty, and crown with honor the great Benefactor, who is too high to be repaid for all his mercies. This deep, undying sentiment of the pious soul, finds utterance in thanksgiving and adoration—in prayer for the extension of the kingdom of Christ, and in all the ways by which a sincere Christian makes manifestation of his piety. But the unwasted, struggling impulse gains strength by all its activities, and longs for new modes of exercise and development. Dissatisfied with the little it can do for the glory of the Saviour, it would gladly give its testimony by suffering. This feeling is natural; and it is strong in every bosom in proportion as piety is profound and intense. It has led many misguided Christians to devote themselves to penances and voluntary inflictions. It led the apostles to rejoice "that they were counted worthy to suffer for Christ." Paul avowed a desire to endure martyrdom for the satisfaction of this profound sentiment, and many early Christians joyfully submitted to the severest tortures as a testimony of their devotion and gratitude to Christ. Not many in these days of peace and toleration are likely to be called to pass through such an ordeal; but if the spirit to suffer the loss of all things for Christ's sake be not still with us, then has the true glory of the church perished with her martyrs. Doubtless this spirit yet lives, and would be made manifest by fitting occasions. Doubtless there are multitudes who would encounter losses of all sorts—privations, labors, and even death itself—for the crucified Redeemer. They remember his words, that if any love father, or mother, or brother, or sister, or houses, or lands, more than him, he cannot be a disciple. They remember that it is often more prudent to lose the life than to save it. Many even feel that they have a baptism to be baptized with, and are straitened till they perform it. They are eager to live, and, if needs be, to die for Christ. They have "put on the Lord Jesus Christ, and made no provision for the flesh, to fulfill the lusts thereof." Their cry is, "Speak, Lord, thy servant heareth." They are not careful to make conditions. Wheresoever God's Spirit or providence will lead, they stand ready to go; neither do they call anything their own which they possess, whether of talent, learning, position, wealth, or influence; but regard themselves only as stewards of the manifold grace of God, and servants to the church for Christ's sake. These are Christians such as Christ came down from heaven to raise up. They are the messengers of his mercy—ministers of grace. Their hearts throb in unison with Christ—their ears are open to every Macedonian cry. The church, this country, the age, and state of the world, want such Christians, and only want enough such, speedily to cover the earth with righteousness.

I have no higher wish on behalf of the young men whom I now address, than to see them thoroughly imbued with the spirit of such a religion as I have attempted to exhibit. Put on, my friends, put ye on the Lord Jesus Christ, and make not provision for the flesh, to fulfill the lusts thereof. I may claim to feel the profoundest interest in your wellfare, but I am not afraid to trust you to the guidance of such auspices. Go forth clad in these robes of purity and beauty, protected by this impenetrable armor of righteousness, and none who love you will have anything to fear or to desire beyond. Christ will guide you aright. Precisely into such positions as are best suited to your talents, and most adapted to usefulness, will he be sure to lead you. And this is the only way for attaining at once the highest happiness and the most perfect development of the intellectual and moral powers. Here you are sure of having "grace sufficient for you," and that is the only sure pledge and hope for eminent success. Here alone you secure that harmony and co-operation of the moral with the mental forces; that concurrence of the emotions with the intellect, indispensable to the fullest development, and the highest achievements, of a human being.

I shall close by making of the exhortation in the text a special application to those who hear me. I am too intimate with the liabilities and the actual history of young men, not to be aware that many of them act in direct opposition to the lessons inculcated in this discourse. They deliberately "*put off* the Lord Jesus Christ," and that for the very purpose of making provision for satisfying the lusts of the flesh. They have found unexpected difficulties in the way of a religious life on their first entrance upon the scenes of public education. The buoyancy and the levity of youth, the confluence of a multitude of petty temptations, small but eager rivalries, new demands upon time, and a new arrangement of their hours, the *esprit du corps* which too often operates to an extent incompatible with an easy discharge of the highest moral duties; these, and many more nameless evils, often combine to test whatever integrity and strength of religious principle and habit the inexperienced youth may have brought from more quiet scenes to the threshold of college life. A brief season of trial, a manly bearing in the face of danger, an honest recurrence to first principles—more than all, humble reliance upon God, and a conscientious observance of the duties of religion, would soon overcome difficulties which are only formidable from their novelty and their number. At this precise point not a few who come among us, with the fairest promise, abandon their religion. Some do it with apparent deliberation, and at once; others gradually, and, it may be, insensibly, but none the less effectually and fatally. A vague purpose is commonly cherished of resuming it again under more favorable auspices, when temptations shall be fewer or weaker, and better helps available. But for the present they put off

Christ, and get their education and form their character without him seeming to regard themselves more free than before to indulge in doubtful pleasures and associations, and still more to omit the distinctive duties and manifestations of a Christian profession. If conscience at first interpose some obstacles in the way of such a defection, it soon accommodates itself with a vicious facility to the cherished inclinations of the heart. I have often seen a hopefully pious youth thus throw away his armor in the day of battle, putting off Christ just when he most needs to put him on—entering on a career of many dangers without religion, just because he thinks it will be difficult or unpleasant to get along with religion. He thus fairly uncovers his bosom to the envenomed shaft. He invites, yea, compels God to forsake him, and then rushes, blind and naked, into the midst of his foes. I speak, young gentlemen, of an experience not unknown among you; not to reproach, but to warn. Some may have gone so far in this downward career, and have drunken so deeply of the cup of cursing which they have chosen, that the voice of affectionate admonition will be lost upon them. Not so, I trust, with others who hear me. The agony is not yet over with them. Shamefully have they slighted, deeply have they grieved, the Saviour; but their hearts yet beat quickly and sorrowfully when they look upon Him whom they have pierced. You who have made a trial of this style in religion, say, Is it satisfactory? Does it shield you in the day of peril? The enjoyments, the lusts of the flesh, for which you have provided at such enormous expense, are they, upon the whole, better than the peace of God and the love of Christ which you have lost? If you look back with desire and self-reproach, then you have still a taste and a conscience for better things, and may, I trust will, rally and struggle to regain the position you have rashly abandoned.

Those who are about to leave this arena of preparation to enter upon new scenes of life, and engage in fresh enterprises, I beseech to listen to the instructions of this occasion. Do not venture to take a step into this dark, troublesome world, now opening before you, without a divine guide. You I may exhort with special emphasis, "Put ye on the Lord Jesus Christ, and make not provision for the flesh, to fulfill the lusts thereof." Fear to move in the grave matter of choosing your profession, and forming the more permanent plans and relations of life, before you assume your proper religious position, and are thus enabled to act under divine direction. You may not neglect this duty without incurring the entire forfeiture of God's promises and grace. Let me inquire of you, with an earnestness and solemnity befitting the importance of the interests involved, whether you have hitherto been true to your convictions of duty, whether your plans of life have thus far been formed prayerfully and conscientiously, in the best moods of your religious feelings, when you most fully appreciated Christ's supreme claims? Are there not in your bosoms half-stifled convictions, slumbering recollections of unpaid vows made under circumstances of deepest solemnity? Look over these archives of conscience with heedful deliberation. Resolutions, formed when your bosoms glowed with zeal and love for Christ, are most likely to be the wisest and the best. Bring yourselves back to the same moral attitude, and review these high, holy purposes, under the same clear manifestations that led to their formation, or you are likely to sin against your own souls irretrievably. "Put ye on the Lord Jesus Christ," and then choose your way under his divine auspices. See to it that you make no provision for the flesh in this deeply interesting crisis of your endless being. For God's sake do not blunder here. Remember you choose for eternity, and that an error at this point must give a wrong direction to all your future career. You determine what you will do for Christ, and for men, and for your own souls. Choose honestly; choose bravely; fearing no labors, or crosses, or sufferings. Better far than honors or crowns are the sacrifices which fidelity to Christ shall impose upon you.

There is among our educated Christian young men a grievous offense, so common as to have become a sign of the times, and so full of evil tendencies as to call loudly for exposure and denunciation. I refer to the levity with which so many treat their early vows of consecration to the Christian ministry. Under convictions of duty and of a heavenly calling, always deeply felt and gratefully recognized in seasons of high religious enjoyment and spiritual devotion, they begin or prosecute their literary career as a preparatory training for the sacred office. With seasons of depression or declension come doubts, and reluctance, and dissatisfaction, with plans of life which really present few alluring aspects to the lukewarm, worldly-minded Christian. Such occasions are often chosen for testing the validity of the call to a work involving many sacrifices, and for which high spirituality and entire consecration to Christ are, confessedly, indispensable qualifications. It is then no difficult task to discover deficiences which the least sensitive conscience must feel, and which there is even a strong temptation to magnify as the means of obtaining a release from obligations hitherto deemed sacred and inviolable. I have briefly indicated the process by which many of our Christian students, designated for the ministry by the most unequivocal marks of a divine vocation, contrive to stifle their own convictions, and elude the sacred claims of the church and of the crucified Saviour. I can truly affirm that no other instances of religious defection and recreancy to sacred duties are wont to fill me with a sorrow so profound and inconsolable. I habitually look upon pious students with the deepest interest, as in a peculiar sense the property of Christ, not only as the purchase of his blood and the trophies of grace, but as the probable and fit instruments to be chosen for the enlargement of his kingdom. It is to be expected that many, so providentially prepared by literary training, should be divinely called to the ministry of reconciliation; and it is matter of unfeigned thankfulness, but none of surprise, that so large a proportion of converted students become deeply impressed with the duty of devoting themselves to this great work. Few, I believe, who maintain a devotional, cross-bearing spirit, ever fall into serious or lasting doubts about the authenticity of their heavenly calling. They may be permitted to pass through seasons of trial and self-examination for the establishment of their faith and for the attainment of a higher moral preparation for the exigences of their holy vocation; but few sincere souls, I am persuaded, will ever be left to discard, as the result of fancy or of enthusiasm, these awful impressions of the highest duty. They who have been seduced by ambition, or indolence, or unbelief, or self-indulgence, from the higher walks of piety, do, indeed, bring upon themselves a moral state to which distrust, and distaste, and absolute repugnance, in regard to their proper mission, are natural and unavoidable. They are no longer fit to be ministers of Christ; but this does not annul their call nor its binding obligations. The burden rests upon them none the less because the strength to bear it is gone. They have clearly fallen into the snare of the devil, and there is only one way of escape. They must revert to first principles, or be irretrievably ruined. They must return to their first love—must revisit the sunny regions of divine grace and manifestation, where clear convictions and holy aspirations domineer over the soul—where love, and faith, and joy in the Holy Ghost impart strength to sustain and light to guide. There is really no other alternative besides such a spiritual revival, for any who lack the nerve, to conclude that they can get along, in life and in death, without a Saviour. To keep this an open question, with some latent floating purpose, to take advantage of a day of feeble impulses and dim manifestation for sliding away into a secular profession, is to impose upon the mind and the heart an intolerable burden, the ominous pledge of comfortless progress, and of ultimate, shameful discomfiture. The interests of both worlds are equally concerned in such a choice of occupation as shall leave the conscience free to approve, and God free to patronize. To those who are rather timid than rebellious, and have still a stronger desire to win the crown than dread of bearing the cross, it may be right to point out the vast resources placed at their disposal, and of which they receive the investiture on assuming their true position; but it must, after all, be admitted to be the mark of a degraded moral tone for a Christian man to manifest much anxiety for anything beyond the doing of his duy. It has been well said that events belong to God; and it may be added, that we are likely to be made happier, as well as better and abler men, by every encounter with difficulties and every blast of adversity. These are God's chosen methods of discipline, and his appointed conditions of all eminent success. So true is this, even in common life, that we do not hesitate to pronounce the most unfavorable auguries of an educated young man, who, in his plans of life, makes an over-careful provision for self-indulgence and an exemption from severe toils and trials. If he will not push from the shore till he has taken pledges for a smooth sea and a favorable breeze—if he must, at all events, have sumptuous fare, and fine linen, and houses of cedar, he insists on conditions which neither Heaven nor earth will grant, and which are wholly incompatible with the performance of great actions, or the formation of great characters. In religion, this timid, selfish spirit, to whatever extent it may exist, is subversive of the best principles of the gospel. It is utterly incompatible with faith, and in itself a mortal sin. We may not inquire too anxiously what Christ will demand of us in return for the blood he has shed and the heaven he has prepared for us; but we know he will have nothing less than entire consecration; and that we are to be ever ready "not only to be bound, but also to die, for the name of the Lord Jesus." It is precisely at this point of entire self-renunciation that the soul becomes endowed with the power of an endless life, and can do all things, through Christ. If this is an excellent attainment, usually reserved for advanced piety and matured graces, it may, nevertheless, become the starting point of every Christian young man. Let him put on the Lord Jesus Christ, and make no provision for the flesh, and he obtains the mastery over all resources, human and divine, needful to the fulfillment of a glorious destiny.

APPENDIX.

NOTE A.—Page 30.

I shall have been greatly misunderstood if it is inferred from the statements and reasonings of this discourse, that I entertain uncharitable views, or would call in question the sincere piety and Christian virtues of the religious denominations of this country. My single object is, to expose a practical and most pernicious error, which is perpetually forced upon my attention by my position, and by some acquaintance with the present condition of the American church. It is no reflection upon the conscientious and devout members of any Christian sect to intimate that persons, attracted to its communion, or its ministry, by other than strictly religious considerations, are not very likely to become eminent for Christian attainments or usefulness. It is well understood, that such proselytes are frequently admitted into their new relations with a degree of distrust and caution, of which no conjecture could be formed from the eclat which is given to their conversions by a sectarian press. In that particular branch of the church which numerically profits most by the tendency I have exposed, a conviction is evidently gaining ground, that it is better policy, upon the whole, to train up its own ministry than to open so wide a door to recruits from the seminaries and pulpits of other denominations. Moderate men are becoming startled at the vaulting speed with which the neophyte so generally hastens to embrace the most extreme opinions and policy known to his new sphere of speculation and activity; while, to considerate men of all parties, it must be obvious, that however a deep, hereditary reverence for imposing forms, and high, exclusive claims, may be compatible with humble, evangelical piety in persons trained, from their childhood, under such influences, there may, at least, be some danger to the unstable, giddy mind of the novice, who, without any such safeguards, is suddenly brought in contact with ideas, to him so new and so magnificent.

I hope I shall not be thought to bestow upon this topic a measure of attention greater than its intrinsic importance. As a practical question, its importance is every day increasing in this country, and the time may not be far away when it will force itself upon the consideration of all thoughtful minds. As a mere sectarian question, it may well enough be regarded as trivial; for it is of little consequence to the enlightened Christian whether the losing party suffer more by mortification than the winning gains by the enjoyment of a petty triumph. There are considerations, however, of far deeper import both to the individual seceder and to the cause of our common Christianity. These easy transitions from the church in which we were reared, or into which we have been providentially led to enter, on our conversion, to another, however pure or orthodox, can hardly ever be effected without injury to the cause of Christ; and I must think them almost never innocent, unless when they are prompted by strictly conscientious motives. It would generally be better to submit to great inconveniences, and even to tolerate slight errors in doctrine or discipline, rather than resort to a remedy so violent and dangerous. To the individual himself it is likely to prove a very hazardous experiment to forsake the hereditary, or the chosen, communion for another. He deprives himself of advantages not to be expected from new religious associations, however pure and elevating. Ties, which religion sanctifies and strengthens for itself, are weakened or broken asunder. The genial sympathies of domestic piety are chilled; the unquestioned authority of hereditary faith is shaken, and all the nameless influences that guard and help a youth, seeking and serving God in the midst of his kindred, and under the approving and watchful eyes of the good men with whose faces and names are associated his hallowed recollections and impressions of the Lord's house, are all utterly lost. I will not affirm that such evils uniformly result from such defections, nor that they are, in all cases, of sufficient force to interfere fatally with the successful prosecution of a religious life. It is no exaggeration, however, to say that they are not of rare occurrence, and that they are wont to exert a very pernicious influence on personal piety.

Evils, of a still graver character than any that befall the individual, are likely to follow such recreancy. In proportion to his position and influence does he inflict upon the church and the general interests of religion the greatest calamity; not chiefly by withdrawing his talents and resources from their appropriate sphere of usefulness, but by grieving pious souls—by awakening distrust of his own sincerity, and resentment for his recreancy, and by provoking uncharitableness, jealousy, sectarianism, and evil-speaking, in multitudes of professing Christians. I have usually been led to doubt whether an influential layman or a minister can ever reasonably expect to do as much good, in any new church relations, as he unavoidably does harm by violating the old. It should be kept in view in estimating the probable effects of such changes, that a man never carries with him into his new field of action more than a small portion of the influence, and other means of usefulness, which he had acquired by faithful services and an upright walk. Of these he is destined to make, at least, a partial forfeiture by the transition, and years must probably elapse before he can regain the vantage ground which he has so lightly abandoned. Suspected, or denounced, by those whom he deserts, he must pass a long probation ere he wins the confidence of his new associates.

Upon the irreligious world the effect of such instability is yet more observable and pernicious. It leads to a distrust of all pretensions to piety, and goes far to confirm the too prevalent suspicion, that when educated or influential men become religious, they have commonly some selfish end to subserve. What gives additional force to such suspicions is the notorious fact that the transition, frequently as it occurs of late, is almost never made where any personal sacrifice, present or prospective, is involved. I do not allow myself to doubt that, in several instances, at least, educated men and ministers have felt constrained to give up old, and contract new, church relations; but I can scarcely recollect a case in which the change was made in the face of losses or sufferings. It is usually from low to higher salaries—from more to less labor or exposure—from less cultivated, or wealthy, or fashionable communities, to those deemed more so. I would not dare express or indulge distrust in regard to the motives which, in any particular instance, may have led to such changes; but the facts to which I have adverted are incontrovertible, as they are universally known. There are few observing or prominent Christians, I apprehend, who have not had some occasion to receive, in silence, the cutting rebukes which irreligious men are accustomed to visit on such transactions. I am free to confess that, in my opinion, no measure of blame or reproaches can possibly transcend the demerits of a man who, for any reasons lower or weaker than such as are strictly conscientious and constraining, puts in jeopardy so many of the precious interests of religion. He betrays a sacred trust. Up to the full measure of his influence, and talents, and position, he inflicts a grievous wrong upon the communion in whose bosom he has been nurtured, or into which he has obtained admission. He diminishes its ability to do good, and casts a doubt on its purity, or orthodoxy. If a minister, set apart and ordained as a teacher of religion, and a dispenser of its holy sacraments, his power to do evil is greatly augmented, and with it the guilt of such a defection. His new investiture of ecclesiastical authority and dignity is equivalent to a public declaration that others are but rash intruders into the sacred office. He thus wounds their reputation and weakens their influence. As far as in him lies, he shakes the confidence of the people in their pastors, and despoils their message of its power over the sinner's conscience. He denies the character and immunities of

Christ's ministers, not to a few obscure individuals, but to nine-tenths of all the consecrated men upon whom the population of this great country depend for religious instruction and consolation. I am ready to admit that conviction may be so clear and controlling as to make it a good man's duty to act in defiance of all these considerations; but no sane mind can, for a moment, hesitate to believe that to do so, on lower grounds, is one of the gravest offenses against religion of which a human being can be guilty.

NOTE B—PAGE 32.

The strong tendency in our religious operations to gather the rich and the poor into separate folds, and so to generate and establish in the church distinctions utterly at variance with the spirit of our political institutions, is the very worst result of the multiplication of sects among us; and I fear it must be admitted that the evil is greatly aggravated by the otherwise benignant working of the voluntary system. Without insisting further upon the probable or possible injury which may befall our free country from this conflict of agencies, ever the most powerful in the formation of national and individual character, no one I am sure, can fail to recognize in this development an influence utterly and irreconcilably hostile to the genius and cherished objects of Christianity. It is the peculiar glory of the gospel, that, even under the most arbitrary governments, it has usually been able to vindicate and practically exemplify the essential equality of man. It has had one doctrine and one hope for all its children; and the highest and the lowest have been constrained to acknowledge one holy law of brotherhood in the common faith of which they are made partakers. Nowhere else, I believe, but in the United States—certainly nowhere else to the same extent—does this antichristian separation of classes prevail in the Christian church. The beggar in his tattered vestments walks the splendid courts of St. Peter's, and kneels at its costly altars by the side of dukes and cardinals. The peasant in his wooden shoes is welcomed in the gorgeous churches of Notre Dame and the Madeline; and even in England, where political and social distinctions are more rigorously enforced than in any other country on earth, the lord and the peasant, the richest and the poorest, are usually occupants of the same church, and partakers of the same communion. That the reverse of all this is true in many parts of this country, every observing man knows full well: and what is yet more deplorable, while the lines of demarkation between the different classes have already become sufficiently distinct, the tendency is receiving new strength and development in a rapidly augmenting ratio. Even in country places, where the population is sparse, and the artificial distinctions of society are little known, the working of this strange element is, in many instances, made manifest, and a petty coterie of village magnates may be found worshiping God apart from the body of the people. But the evil is much more apparent, as well as more deeply seated, in our populous towns, where the causes which produce it have been longer in operation, and have more fully enjoyed the favor of circumstances. In these great centres of wealth, intelligence, and influence, the separation between the classes is, in many instances, complete, and in many more the process is rapidly progressive. There are crowded religious congregations composed so exclusively of the wealthy as scarcely to embrace an indigent family or individual; and the number of such churches, where the gospel is never preached to the poor, is constantly increasing. Rich men, instead of associating themselves with their more humble fellow Christians, where their money as well as their influence and counsels are so much needed, usually combine to erect magnificent churches, in which sittings are too expensive for any but people of fortune, and from which their less-favored brethren are as effectually and peremptorily excluded as if there were dishonor or contagion in their presence. A congregation is thus constituted, able, without the slightest inconvenience, to bear the pecuniary burdens of twenty churches, monopolizing and consigning to comparative inactivity intellectual, moral, and material resources, for want of which so many other congregations are doomed to struggle with the most embarrassing difficulties. Can it for a moment be thought, that such a state of things is desirable, or in harmony with the spirit and design of the gospel?

A more difficult question arises when we inquire after a remedy for evils too glaring to be overlooked, and too grave to be tolerated without an effort to palliate, if not to remove them. The most obvious palliative, and one which has already been tried to some extent by wealthy churches or individuals, is the erection of free places of worship for the poor. Such a provision for this class of persons would be more effectual in any other part of the world than in the United States. Whether it arises from the operation of our political system, or from the easy attainment of at least the prime necessaries of life, the poorer classes here are characterized by a proud spirit, which will not submit to receive even the highest benefits in any form that implies inferiority or dependence. This strong and prevalent feeling must continue to interpose serious obstacles in the way of these laudable attempts. If in a few instances churches for the poor have succeeded in our large cities, where the theory of social equality is so imperfectly realized in the actual condition of the people, and where the presence of a multitude of indigent foreigners tends to lower the sentiment of independence so strong in native-born Americans, the system is yet manifestly incapable of general application to the religious wants of our population. The same difficulty usually occurs in all attempts to induce the humbler classes to worship with the rich in sumptuous churches by reserving for their benefit a portion of the sittings free, or at a nominal rent. A few only can be found who are willing to be recognized and provided for as beneficiaries and paupers, while the multitude will always prefer to make great sacrifices in order to provide for themselves in some humbler fane. It must be admitted that this subject is beset with practical difficulties, which are not likely to be removed speedily, or without some great and improbable revolution in our religious affairs. Yet if the respectable Christian denominations most concerned in the subject shall pursue a wise and liberal policy for the future, something may be done to check the evil. They may retard its rapid growth, perhaps, though it will most likely be found impossible to eradicate it altogether. It ought to be well understood, that the multiplication of magnificent churches is dayly making the line of demarkation between the rich and the poor more and more palpable and impassable. There are many good reasons for the erection of such edifices. Increasing wealth and civilization seem to call for a liberal and tasteful outlay in behalf of religion, yet is it the dictate of prudence no less than of duty to balance carefully the good and the evil of every enterprise. It should ever be kept in mind, that such a church virtually writes above its sculptured portals an irrevocable prohibition to the poor, "Procul o procul este profani."

I will not pretend to determine how far it might be wise, even if it were practicable, to check the liberal spirit now so active in multiplying sumptuous religious edifices. We have perhaps more encouragement to look in another direction for the melioration desired. There can be no doubt that a general increase of humble, spiritual religion would operate as a powerful check upon the prevailing disposition to prefer communion with opulent congregations, rather than pursue the walks of a lowlier piety in company with the poor. The same good ends would be further promoted by the increasing prevalence of a liberal catholic spirit. A decided and simultaneous advance in piety and charity, though it should stop short of harmonizing conflicting sects and opinions, and bringing their votaries to worship in a common temple, might yet be sufficient to reach and considerably mitigate some of the greatest hardships to which I have adverted. In such an improved state of Christian sentiment, a congregation, or a sect, opulent in intellectual or pecuniary means, beyond the ratio of its numbers, might easily confer the greatest benefits on the feeble and destitute. A wealthy denomination with few of the poor under its ministry, and with little access to this class, would then be inclined to aid those who are providentially called to preach the gospel to the masses. How easily might one of our great metropolitan churches relieve a dozen poor congregations from the burden of debts, or other embarrassments,

6

under which they are left to struggle on from year to year! What inestimable benefits might a denomination, at once the smallest and richest, confer by aiding the poorer sects in extending the blessings of religion and education to the vast multitude placed by divine Providence under their influence and watchcare! Now it can hardly be doubted, that with such an enlargement of charity as I have supposed, there would come more enlarged views of duty and privilege, and that sectarian lines might cease to be insuperable barriers in the way of a far more exuberant and diffusive liberality than now prevails. Under such better auspices it would at least be no longer possible for opulent, enlightened Christian denominations to look with hostility or even indifference upon their fellow-laborers in the vineyard of a common Master. The sympathies as well as the resources of the whole Christian church would look about in quest of its wants and substantial interests: while there would inevitably arise bonds of brotherhood, so many and so strong, between all the members of the one Christian family, as would go far to exclude all the petty jealousies and heart-burnings which wealth and position are sure to provoke in the church no less than in the world, when they forget their proper mission.

One lesson more, we should imagine, would be ineffaceably impressed upon those Christian denominations which, through providential means or their own special adaptations and exertions, monopolize a large portion of the influential classes, while they have signally failed of obtaining a corresponding development among the great body of the people. It is a lesson of enlarged catholic liberality. They have, in their relative position, a clear demonstration at least that others as well as they have a dispensation of the gospel committed to them. That, surely, cannot be the *only* apostolic and legitimate system of faith or polity, which, after an experiment carried through successive generations of men, has, in this country, shown itself essentially incapable of penetrating the masses. They who evangelize the wealthy, the intellectual, and the refined, do unquestionably perform a good work; and there may be those who have a special vocation to this inviting field. No liberal-minded Christian will undervalue their efforts, or desire to call in question the genuineness of their piety, or the validity of their ecclesiastical system; but it may be well for all parties to remember that there are signs of apostleship older and surer than this mission to the rich; and they need not despair of making good their claim to a part in this ministry who can appeal, as their Master did, to eminent success among the masses, and affirm, like him, that through their instrumentality "the blind receive their sight and the lame walk, the lepers are cleansed and the deaf hear, the dead are raised up and THE POOR HAVE THE GOSPEL PREACHED UNTO THEM."

www.ingramcontent.com/pod-product-compliance
Lightning Source LLC
LaVergne TN
LVHW021407110826
845150LV00007B/1823